Good Luck!

Taya Chandell

CW00571281

This page is intentionally left blank.

SCRIBBLES AND STORIES

A Compilation of Stories and
Some Mostly True Experiences

By Layne Wardell

Scribbles and Stories

Layne Wardell

Photo by Taylor Brandon and Simeon Jacobson on Unsplash.

ISBN-10: 8 83941 630 7

ISBN-13: 979 8 83941 630 7

Printed in USA.

Dedicated to

My mom, Dawna Rae Hall Wardell

Contents

Prologue

I decided to print some of the same stories from volumes one and two, leaving those of a personal nature out and adding more that I wrote since the printing of volume two.

The first story is a tribute to my mom who always seemed to find enough time for each of us kids while we were growing up as well as anyone else who might need a little help. She's an amazing woman whose faith in God is an inspiration to me as well as many others she has come in contact with through the years. Often times we would come home from school to the great smell of some sugary dessert, only to watch as it marched out the door destined to go to some family who was sick or needed a little extra love and kindness. She's truly a Saint. Thanks, Mom!

Other stories about the Easter Bunny, lost ropes, skunks, my first bronc ride, horse stories, prairie dog roping, a flying mountain man, and others will hopefully keep the reader entertained and maybe even provoke a thought or two.

Thanks for reading!

Layne

CHAPTER I

Mom

My mom is a pretty incredible lady. She and Dad were married just before they both graduated from high school. She's the last of six children by nine years, all growing up on the family farm up Dry Fork Canyon, just north of Vernal, Utah. She and her siblings were the fourth generation of the Hall family to live there. It was one of the oldest homesteads in the canyon.

She and Dad raised five kids after losing two others as babies. Dad was gone a lot due to his work. He was a pipeline welder and that job took him all over the western United States, sometimes for months at a time. That made it kind of tough on her at times.

She was always frugal and looking for ways to be as self-sufficient as possible, much to our dismay at times. We kids suffered through cracked wheat cereal, some goopy stuff she called gluten that I think was supposed to take the place of bread, fruit leather (*I happened to like that!*) and, when we were out of butter or margarine, we would use bacon grease instead. She even made a fake apple pie out of Ritz crackers a few times. Put enough sugar in about anything and it'll taste just fine. Most of the time, dessert was jam or jelly on bread with butter and or peanut butter. We really looked forward to Thanksgiving and Christmas because that's when we would have a lot of pie. She would make each of us a cake for our birthdays, too.

I remember having toast and warm milk quite a few times for supper. I liked it. I know it doesn't sound too good to some people, but she used homemade bread so it didn't get mushy as fast as store-bought bread and she used a lot of butter. Sometimes, she would get out a cookie sheet and make cinnamon toast in the oven. The sugar and cinnamon would be all crispy and good!

Dad still had a few sheep and would butcher a mutton every now and then. The first thing that got cooked were the ribs in the oven broiler. You had to eat them quickly or the grease would stick to the roof of your mouth. Dad didn't allow any waste, either: "Don't stare at it, eat it!"

You ate everything but the bone. I remember going into the bathroom after eating and literally scraping the grease out of my mouth.

She would also fix us poached eggs for breakfast sometimes. They were kind of like a soft boiled egg. I would chop mine up with my fork and add salt, pepper and some butter. I liked them that way.

Speaking of poached food, we ate a lot of fresh buckskin most of the year. (*A lot of people these days just say deer, but I grew up calling it buckskin.*) We usually had around 200 deer in the fields every night so it didn't bother us to pick one off to eat every now and then. Dad could clean one out in less than five minutes and proved it once when he and Mom were driving downriver to the Ranch one evening. Dad had just killed a deer next to the road and, as he started to clean it out, they could hear a vehicle coming toward them. Thankfully, the roads weren't very good back then so everyone drove slowly. This gave Dad just enough time to clean it out and throw it in the back of the truck before getting caught. Mom said it took less than five minutes from start to finish and that was in the dark!

Sometimes we would get visitors stop by the Ranch to visit. One time, the game warden stopped by. His last name was Fullenwider. I can't remember his first name...maybe "Officer". Anyway, he stopped by and had been there for quite a while when Mom decided it was time to start fixing supper and invited him to stay and eat. After realizing how long he'd been there, he politely declined and headed out the door. About that same time, Mom was dragging a deer leg out from under the bed. As she started cutting meat off for cooking, she realized she would have done it right in front of the game warden! Kinda scared her. She said that she 'fessed up a while later to him and asked him what he'd of done. He told her that he would have enjoyed a good meal! Quite a bit different now!

She sewed most of our clothes. Our jeans were store bought, but a lot of the other stuff we wore came from her sewing machine. She wasn't afraid to let us learn how to use it, either. I don't remember anyone ever sewing themselves to anything. We were pretty careful. She also ironed everything. Five kids kept her pretty busy! We learned how to iron clothes early on, too.

We had to haul all our water from town. We had a big cistern that would hold enough water to last a couple weeks if we weren't wasteful. If Dad was home, we weren't wasteful! When I was pretty young I remember one night

I needed to use the bathroom and was doing my thing when Dad hollered at me to shut off the water!

"Sorry Dad, I can't!"

We all used the same bath water. We didn't flush the toilet every time either, unless there were solids. I was always amazed at how wasteful people in town were with their water!

Most years just before school started, she would go to Grand Junction (*about two hours away*) to buy our clothes for the coming year. We always looked forward to getting new clothes, but one time she came back with nothing. While she was paying for the clothes, a thief grabbed them and got away. We had no more money for anything else and Dad was a long ways away. She knelt down and told God her troubles and asked for help. She had no other ideas or means. A day or so later, Dona Brady showed up with a box full of clothes and every item fit one of us kids. We didn't care that they were used; we were grateful for clothes that didn't have holes in them!

Up until 1976, we lived in a place that was only about a mile and a half from town. Even being that close to town, we never wasted a trip. Gas cost money and that was something we didn't have any extra of. When I was around eight or nine years old, Dad decided to start farming the Ranch again. He and my older brother, Barry, would use pitchforks to throw the hay into the back of the truck while my younger sister, Punk, or I would steer the truck while looking through the steering wheel. I remember Dad telling me to push the clutch in to stop the truck, but, if I needed to stop it quickly, to push on the brake. Well, being a little kid, I got a little bored and wanted to do something different so the next time he hollered at me to stop, I used the brake and killed the truck. Punk was on the top of the hay and, when the truck stopped so suddenly, she fell on her belly and was doing an admirable impression of a monkey by digging her fingers and feet into the hay while hanging upside down a few feet above a blow snake! Yeah, I got hollered at for it, but it's still funny! I got hollered at quite often.

We usually had a pretty big garden. There were some people from town that reaped rewards from our garden by driving the 13 miles down the road every now and then. We never caught them. We also got a herd of young cows about 1974.

Mom was a pretty good cowboy in addition to the other hundred chores she had to do. If you look at her fingers, you'll notice that they don't all go in the same direction. She got bucked off once and kinda messed 'em up. One time, she was riding a buckskin horse of Barry's called Buck. It was springtime and the river was a little high. That never scared her before as we all knew horses will swim if needed. All horses except for Buck that is. He lost his footing and panicked. Mom fell off and he tried to use her for a raft, nearly knocking her out and almost drowning her. Dad happened to be watching and drug her out of the river. Buck drowned. Dad's brother, Tom, was down the river a few miles and was able to catch the floating horse and retrieve the saddle and bridle.

We had some chickens when we finally moved back to the Ranch full time. There was an old chicken coop that my grandpa had built that we were using. They'd used straw bales with boards on the inside and outside for the walls so the straw was the insulation between the boards. Now, this had been around for quite a while and the hens had a nest in the straw that you had to reach up into to get the eggs. You had to just reach in and feel for the eggs because you couldn't see them. Dad and I were working on some project in the yard while Mom was gathering the eggs and doing her morning chores. Suddenly, we hear her holler and the next thing we see is Mom running to the house saying, "Eww! Eww! Eww!!"

She wasn't just running, she would run a couple steps and then hop while shaking both her hands and her head! She kept this pattern up until she nearly made it to the house. We finally got her to stop and tell us what was going on. Well, she'd reached into the nest and grabbed hold of a blow snake instead of an egg! I swear, it's still one of the funniest memories I have of her! Run, hop, run, hop, Eww! Eww! Sorry Mom, but it was funny! It still brings tears to my eyes just thinking about it! It's sure a good thing that she's always been such a good sport!

Another good and favorite story of mine is when she got sick. Dad would have a drink every now and then and had a bottle of whiskey stashed in his truck. Mom was feeling pretty rough and still had all us kids to take care of. She'd heard that a hot toddy would make you feel better if you were sick. Some people claimed it made them feel better even if they weren't sick! She wasn't exactly sure what went into such a drink or how much of what, but she was going to do the best she knew how. Anyway, she went out and found the bottle then poured herself a half glass full and topped it off with water, threw in some butter, warmed it up on the stove and drank it. She said it made her feel so good that she had another! She went to bed and went right to sleep. The next morning she woke up feeling great! She didn't even get a hangover! I don't know if she ever tried another after that, or not.

Family Home Evenings were a hassle for all of us. We were supposed to set one evening aside for instruction and learning, geared toward the spiritual part of our life. Being kids, we had other things that were more interesting than sitting around and having a lesson every Monday night, but I remember this one. She gave each of us kids a thread. We tied our thread to the handle of a cast iron frying pan and tried to lift it up. The thread always broke. Then she had us all do it together and we were able to lift the pan without any trouble. The lesson was: we need each other. There are some things we can do on our own, but in order to make it through life, we need to help and be helped by others...especially family members. I've never forgotten it.

All in all, we had everything we needed; maybe not all we wanted, but that ended up being a blessing. Many who read this might think that we were deprived of a lot of what they consider necessities. We weren't. We were blessed with not as much as others so that later on, we would be grateful with having enough. Too many people don't know the difference between needs and wants. They watch television and believe the advertisers when they are told that they "deserve" this or that product. When we go to mountain man rendezvous, we have what we call Mountain Man toilet paper for sale. It's inner bark from a cottonwood tree or if we're out of that, cedar bark. The looks of recoil and disgust we get from some (*especially the young*) is priceless. They can't imagine being so crude as to resort to using such stuff as that! I can promise you that I have used worse. So would they if they had to. Others get a chuckle out of it and some even buy some to give away as a joke. And just like the toilet paper we use in the house, it can be used as a fire starter too!

CHAPTER 2

Stories

Cuff Words

One day when our son was still pretty young, we were driving home from church and my wife asked him what his class lesson was about.

"Cuff words," he said.

"Cuff words?"

"Yeah, we're not supposed to say cuff words."

I asked him if he knew any cuff words and he said he didn't.

How are you supposed to know what not to say if you don't know what not to say? Slow as my mind works, I thought I realized what the "cuff words" were.

"Did your teacher say "cuff words" or "cuss words," I asked him.

He wasn't sure. I was pretty sure she never used cuss words in her class, but I'm not sure to this day what cuff words are or were, but I've never heard him say cuss words! Thanks to good Primary teachers and a great mom!

The Easter Bunny

Work was kind of hard to come by for a while so I went to work at the local grocery store cutting meat. It wasn't bad except in the spring time when things were greening up and I really wanted to be outside. There were some bright spots, though. One of those was a little girl that would come to the store with her grandma. She was the daughter of a girl I remembered from high school who was a couple years younger than me.

Anyway, when a box of cookies got smashed or broken, we would put the remains in a cookie jar and give them to the kids when they came by. She was a regular customer and we were pretty good buddies. One day she came in and had an announcement to make.

"Sunday, I'm gonna be four!" she said as she held up four little fingers.

I congratulated her on her soon to come birthday and then she had another announcement. "Sunday the Easter bunny is coming!"

Well, I hope I'm a better person now as opposed to what I was then, because it cost me a friend. The things older people joke around about are sometimes serious business to little kids. What I thought was a funny ended up crushing my poor, young friend. "No he's not, the rabbit hunters got him last winter," I said.

Her eyes got big, her mouth dropped open and she spun around and ran to her grandma. She never came back.

Pet Skunks?

Up until the summer of 1976, we lived about a mile and a half north of town. We had some neighbors close by and some of the kids were about the same age as a couple in our family. I was over visiting when one of the older sons came home carrying two or three seemingly harmless baby skunks.

They would fit in an adult's hand and didn't seem to be afraid. They were set down on the kitchen floor in front of the cat food dish enjoying a free meal. Everybody was saying how cute they were and they were cute, but I also knew they were fully loaded. When it comes to defense, I've heard it said that porcupines are "open carry" and skunks are "concealed carry".

When I saw their Siamese cat come in, I started for the door. Everybody was concentrating on the skunks and didn't see the cat. The cat was on full alert now, both ears forward, tail twitching back and forth and stalking toward his dish to defend his territory! Time to run the trespassers off! About the time I got the door open, I heard a "whoosh!" followed by wails of anguish, agony and despair! I didn't go to visit for quite a while after that! I don't know what happened to the skunks, but I never saw them again.

Trouble at School

When I was in high school, we had to go to the grade school for school lunch. Since the grade school was just down the hill from the high school, we always walked to it. One of my buddies was named Dave and we generally hung around each other quite a bit. One day as we were walking down the hill on our way to eat, there were a couple small freshman boys in front of us going to have lunch. We were seniors and generally left people alone. Dave was never mean, but he would joke around with people every now and then. He saw an opportunity to have some fun and turned to me and told me to watch. He trotted down the hill and caught one boy by the belt, picked him up with one arm and carried him like a suitcase the rest of the way down the hill at a trot. We thought it was hilarious until the little twerp started calling him all kinds of filthy names. Then it got a little serious. Dave outweighed this kid by about 90 pounds and I watched Dave cock his arm back like he was going to punch the little punk. I could visualize his head getting splattered all over the green grass and thought, "Oh NO!" Dave caught his head in the crook of his arm, kind of like a nut cracker.

The next thing I saw were arms and legs flailing around like a bug. THAT was funny! Dave let him go just as I got there and of course I was laughing because it was funny again! Then the little twerp turned on me and repeated all the vile things to me that he'd been calling Dave a little earlier. Well, I only outweighed him by about 30 pounds and wasn't going to stand for that nonsense either. I made a fist with my right hand and rapped his forehead with my middle knuckle. His eyes teared up and said he was going to tell the principal. We told him to go ahead and we went on our way then ate our lunch.

After we finished lunch, we went to the principal's office and waited on the steps outside his door. The principal finally came out and was surprised to see us waiting for him. He told Dave to come in and started to turn away. I said, "What about me?!"

He told me to get out of there!

After Dave was turned loose, he told me that evidently this kid had gotten several guys in trouble for picking on him due to his small size. His Mode of Operation was to mouth off to them enough that they, like me, had had enough and pounded on him a little. The principal had had enough of this and told him so. According to Dave, the punk was told by the principal that he (*the principal*) didn't care if they killed him (*the punk*)! Well, that seemed to cure the problem. Years later I was told by a coworker that the guy told him that I was a mean guy! Funny!

Aunt Attack

My mother-in-law and her family grew up in Weld County, Colorado. It's on the northeastern plains of the state. She has 11 siblings who all married and have children so there's a pretty good pile of them.

Every year they have a family reunion on the homestead and it's usually well attended. We just happened to be enjoying ourselves at said reunion when a particular aunt happened to walk by. (*Now she had made sure that she and her husband attended our son's Eagle Scout court of honor, which was no small thing to do on their part. They live about seven hours away. It was quite a sacrifice for them to make and showed how much they thought of our son.*) Anyway, with that background you can understand a little why she asked the question that she posed to me at that point. "Layne, I am your favorite aunt, aren't I?"

Now keep in mind that at the time the question was asked, I was surrounded by several aunts. Not just any aunts; these grew up using guns and knives! I thought highly of all of them and was wondering how to get out of that crocodile pit unscathed! When the question was asked I felt all those sets of eyes swivel and lock on me like a guided nuclear missile.

Every day I pray for help and guidance in the things I do and the things I will be exposed to. If I ever needed inspiration, it was now. "Yup," I responded, "Now what was your name?"

Well, she said something about me being ornery and left! I breathed a big sigh of relief and came out of that one in one original piece! God answers prayers if we're willing to listen.

Mighty Hunters

While guiding hunters years ago, I had some interesting experiences. This is one of them.

I had two men from Texas that wanted to be elk hunters. They paid their fees, bought their licenses, brought their rifles and even brought the proper ammunition to go with their guns. This was their first elk hunt and I don't think they realized how strenuous an elk hunt can be or the challenges involved with most successful hunts.

We found a couple bulls for them to shoot at the first day. One guy shot six times and his brother-in-law shot seven times. The elk just walked away. WALKED away! Completely unscathed and apparently not too bothered.

The next day it had snowed a couple inches which made it perfect for tracking. My hunter and I cut a track of what I thought was a young bull so we started following it. The tracks led to a steep timbered hillside and as I looked over the edge, there stood a young three point bull about 30 yards away. For some reason that I can't remember, the mighty hunter had wandered off a little and couldn't see me or the bull. When he couldn't see me, he panicked and started hollering my name, effectively scaring off the bull.

The next day, we decided to come into the area a different way. We needed to walk across a bare spot on a fairly steep hillside. That's when we found out my mighty hunter was afraid of heights. He almost locked up in the middle of the hillside. I talked him into coming on across since he had just as far to go if he turned around and went back. That ruined the hunt for them. It didn't matter that they had more chances to kill an elk than 75% of the rest of Colorado hunters had, not to mention that two of the bulls were really good six points. In their mind, I was a terrible guide and they couldn't wait to tell everybody.

I always carried some candy with me to snack on while hunting. I happened to have some chocolate covered raisins and then had what I thought was a scathingly brilliant idea. I was walking in front of my mighty hunter and happened to have some raisins in my hand when we came across some elk droppings. I reached down, acting like I scooped up some poop and showed my hand just long enough for him to see I had something in it, then popped them in my mouth. Well, it was priceless! His eyes got big as he watched me chew it up. "Yup, about two days old," I said.

His mouth dropped open and when he saw me swallow them, he about lost it! He got mad! I laughed! They went home empty handed and at that point, it didn't really bother me. It's tough when you work your tail off trying to please people who are clueless as to how much work it takes to make them happy and successful, and it's never enough. I don't miss baby sitting hunters at all.

CHAPTER 3

Climbing the Mountain

"Is it really worth it?" I asked the question out loud, not to anyone in particular. Mostly to myself I guess, since I was alone at the foot of this mountain. I couldn't tell how high the mountain was from where I was at and I wasn't sure what was at the top either. All I knew was what I'd been told by others. They claimed that there was a lodge on top that would surpass anything else on earth. The food was the best there was, the vistas unrivaled, and the staff was supposed to be out of this world. Basically, it was there to provide all a person needed to be happy.

"It must have cost a pretty penny to put something like that together," I thought.

"That's right, the cost is unimaginable ," someone answered. Startled, I spun around to see who spoke, not realizing that I'd been thinking out loud.

"Who are you?" I didn't recognize the man, but something about him seemed familiar to me.

"I am here to help you find your way up this mountain," he replied without telling me his name.

"We need to get moving if you're going to make it to the top before dark," he said.

"But it's still early morning! ," I complained.

"If you plan on making it at all, we need to be o our way. If it gets too late, you won't have enough light to find your way up."

"Have you been there? I've never talked to anyone who's ever been there, or even anyone who even claims to have been there. How do I know you're not going to get me lost and leave me when I need help?"

"If you will follow my instructions, you will learn to have confidence and faith in my guidance and even protection as time goes by."

"Wait! You said protection! Protection from what?"

"I did. Journeys like this with rewards like what await successful travelers always have certain perils and risks to deal with."

"You mentioned something about the high cost earlier. How much will it cost me to go to this supposed Valhalla?"

"If you make it to the top, the cost has already been paid. We need to get moving or you'll not have to worry about it. Let's go!" He motioned for me to take the lead with his right hand and I started into the brush on a little used trail.

"Wait! Aren't you supposed to be my guide? Aren't guides supposed to lead the way?"

"I'm a silent guide. If the path or way you take leads you in the wrong direction, I'll tap you on your shoulder but it's up to you to listen and make the decisions. Always remember that the more good decisions you make, the easier it will be to make more good decisions and make it to the top. If you come to a spot you're not clear on, just ask for help."

With that, we headed into what, for me, was the great unknown. The grade wasn't steep, but there was plenty of brush to deal with. Some of it was so thick that I had to back out and find a new route several times. As long as I kept going uphill I knew I was headed in the right direction. It didn't take long before I found others who were on their own way up the mountain. Some were still excited about the journey while others were already discouraged. I noticed that all had a guide somewhere around them. Those who were excited were those who had a guide right by them. Those whose guides hung back were the discouraged ones. That made sense to me and I was glad my guide stayed close by. I mentioned to my guide that I was grateful that I had a better guide than those who were discouraged and unhappy with their journey. "The reason they're unhappy isn't because they have a poor guide. It's because they don't listen to their guide. They get lost, scratched and scraped up when, if they would ask their guide for help instead of being prideful and hard headed, they'd be better off."

It wasn't long after that, that we came to a big patch of dark timber and the ground dropped off into a canyon that I hadn't realized was even there. The dim trail we followed seemed to go right into it. I turned to my guide and found that he was closer than he had ever been before. When I asked him why he was so close, he replied that we needed to stay close to make it through this dark section.

We hadn't gone far when I could hear someone calling for help. The voice came from deeper in the canyon. As I started toward the voice, I felt a couple taps on my shoulder. "But someone needs help! I need to go down to show them the way back up! Where is their guide, anyway?"

"Their guide is up on the trail, where we need to stay. Call to that person so they can come up to you."

It took a while, but eventually the voice got closer and finally turned into a young man. He was scared and his face showed the fear and worry that comes from being lost.

"I was about to give up," he said. "I'm so glad you came and guided me back, I'd nearly lost any hope that I would ever make it back. Everything is a terrible, tangled mess down there and it is so dark that I couldn't see. I couldn't tell which way was up or down and I was afraid to move for fear of getting even more lost!"

"Why didn't you listen to your guide?"

"I was so tired of him tapping me on my shoulder that I decided that I could find my own way. I started out just fine, but when I tripped and fell down the hill, I couldn't make it back up and HE wouldn't come help!"

"When you stop listening to me as your guide, you are moving away from me. I'm not leaving you," said his guide. "There are places that we're not allowed to go and when you go to those places, you're on your own."

The young man's name was Randy and he was full of confidence in himself. Now that he was back on the right track, he took the lead. Shortly we noticed a dim light in front of us. This was followed up with more lights in the darkness. Soon there were so many lights that it looked like stars in the night sky. This one soon turned into a camp fire next to the trail. a group of men and women were sitting next to it enjoying cool beverages and the welcoming light in the darkness. The inviting warmth and light of the fire beckoned us to stay, but the bawdy talk and drunkenness made me want to keep going. After Randy's harrowing experience earlier, he accepted a man's invitation to stop and join them for a while. Randy's guide again tapped him on his shoulder which just seemed to irritate Randy. "I have plenty of time to make it up this mountain. Just let me stay here for a little while and then I'll head out."

His guide backed away to wait.

As I watched this exchange, I decided to part company with Randy. So on our way Tonto and I went, leaving Randy and a disappointed guide behind. (*Oh, since my guide wouldn't tell me his name, I named him Tonto which he took with some faint amusement tickling the corners of his mouth and eyes.*) After a while, the trees started to open up and let some light in. Tonto gave me some space and up the mountain we went. According to the position of the sun, it was still morning and I still couldn't see the top of the mountain. Maybe it really was going to take most of the day, after all. The grade got steeper the further we went until I had to grasp the branches of the brush just to keep going. Every time I looked back, there was Tonto following along, although it didn't seem like he was having as much trouble as I was. We finally topped out on a small bench or plateau. I was tired!

The sweat was burning my eyes and running down my back. I needed a rest so I sat down on a fallen tree for a break. That's when I realized that I was far from alone. There were people all over the place. Hundreds, maybe even thousands it seemed were here on this plateau. I noticed several other people in a group were also taking advantage of the respite from the climb.

They called to me to come over and enjoy some cool water from a spring they were sitting next to. It sounded good to me, so I took them up on it. The water was cold and refreshing. Soon I was invigorated enough to be on my way. Several encouraged me to stay longer and enjoy the view and company. They'd been there quite a while and didn't seem to be inclined to go any further.

"Look around you! This is a great place, the view, the cool green grass, the fresh water, shade under the trees and US! There really isn't any place better on this mountain than what you see here! There can't be!"

"Have any of you been any further up the mountain than this?"

"No, but look around you! There's no way it gets better than this! We've watched others go on by but they came back. They said it just turns to lava rock that lizards don't even live on. Face it, do you really believe there's a place on top of this mountain that people say is the equal of heaven on earth? From what others have said, it's more like hell! Only a fool would leave this place to chase a fable that just can't be true!"

Tap, tap, tap. Tonto was moving away from me with a questioning look in his eyes, but saying nothing.

"Is what these people telling me true? They have witnesses that say there's nothing but desert up there!"

"Who are you talking to? Maybe you got a little more fried than you thought! You need to sit down and have a little more water and cool down. No reason to hurry off. Take some more time like the rest of us."

I looked around again and noticed that none of these people had a guide even close to them and they evidently couldn't see Tonto. About that time an attractive and provocative young woman came up to me and took my hand in hers. "You don't really want to leave us, do you? I would love to get better acquainted with you, and I can't if you leave!"

She looked deep into my eyes and smiled a surprisingly disarming smile. My knees went weak, my heart started racing and I got sweaty all over again.

I tried to speak and all that came out was a barely discernible, "Nnnnyaahh!".

She giggled and said something about that being cute as she led me back toward the group. I looked for Tonto. He was there where I'd left him, his eyes piercing my soul. Where I had left HIM! He wasn't leaving me, I was leaving him! I remembered Randy and his ordeals. I gathered up some courage and stopped.

"Look, I've enjoyed your company and you've all made me feel welcome, but I need to find out for myself. Thanks for the offer, I really appreciate it,"

"You stupid FOOL!" The words were spoken with so much feeling that it made me wonder if she could ever be true to anyone who had any thoughts different from her own. At that point, it seemed that there was so much venom inside her that I was surprised the very grass under her feet didn't spontaneously combust! Evidently she was pretty used to getting her own way. "You'll be back, just like everybody else, but don't expect to stay here with us! Get lost, loser!" Well, so much for a romantic relationship today!

I found Tonto where I'd left him and we continued on our way. They were right. Soon the cool green of the mountain turned to hot rocks and dirt with not a plant or wildlife anywhere to be seen. Just heat and lava rock as far as I could see, which wasn't very far because of the heat waves. It wasn't long before the lava was doing a number on my boots and hands. I was glad I'd filled up on water before this part as I was getting parched. I looked back at Tonto. He hadn't had much to say since the plateau, not that he said much anyway. He just nodded with his head to keep going. The heat was stifling. It was getting harder just to keep moving. I was dehydrating quickly and if I didn't find some relief soon, bad things were going to happen.

"You stupid FOOL!" It kept coming back over and over again until I was beginning to believe it. Was this how I was going to die? It sure felt like it. I looked at Tonto and saw a glint of compassion in his eyes as he nodded to continue forward. My vision was getting blurry and I was starting to stagger a little. There wasn't a spot of shade anywhere around that I could see. I desperately needed some relief from this terrible, stifling heat that seemed to be sucking the life from my body. I thought back on my life and wondered if I was going to heaven or hell. They were right, this was as close to what I'd read hell was as I could think of. Finally, I could go no further and collapsed. I would die in this pile of hot rocks. I had nothing left. I could barely speak and tried to ask Tonto why he led me here and to let my family know what happened and where to find me, but all that came out was a raspy whisper.

Then came the clouds. The shade was better, but the rocks still held the heat. Lightly at first, then came the rain. I could have sworn that there was steam coming off those rocks, they were so hot! My body actually felt like it was soaking up the rain water as it fell on me. I opened my mouth to catch any and all raindrops I could. Then it was over…the rain, anyway. It was still cloudy and after a while I was able to move around a little. I regained my sight and balance and wondered how Tonto was doing and if he'd made it out or not. He was sitting on a rock behind me looking like nothing had happened. Amazing!

Now that the air had cooled down to a manageable temperature, the heat waves were gone and I could see greenery in the distance. I'd nearly made it all across the lava field but didn't know it. We were almost out of the rock pile when something caught my eye. I wasn't sure what it was, but it looked like a hand. I looked at Tonto and he nodded toward it so that's where we went.

Sure enough, the hand was still attached to an arm that was also attached to a body. That body was still alive and looked to be an older woman. The hair was all straggly and the hands were thrashed by the same rocks that had nearly killed me. How in the world did an old woman make it this far I wondered? Then she looked up. She wasn't old at all, just beaten down by the heat. She was actually in better shape than I was and was using one hand to cup rain water out of a depression in the rock to drink while supporting herself with the one I'd spotted.

"Are you okay?" I asked.

"I am now. I was getting pretty beaten before the rain came. Are you on your way up the mountain?"

"I am. Do you have any idea how much further it is?"

"Not really, but my guide says I can still make it before dark if I keep moving.

"Would you mind if I try to keep up with you?"

"Well, it looks like you caught up with me. You shouldn't have any trouble keeping up. I might have trouble keeping up with you!" Her smile was a warm and welcome thing to see. She seemed to have a strong inner beauty that defied her current appearance. She was, I decided, a lady. Not all women are ladies, although all ladies are women.

Ladies have a quiet reverence about them that separates them from women. They are more than women. Ladies can have calluses and wear ragged clothes and still be ladies. Women can be stunningly beautiful and physically attractive on the outside, but like the woman at the spring, full of jealousy, hate and selfishness on the inside. That beautiful woman was not a lady.

This lady was a good traveling companion. She was tougher than me, I decided. She possessed a mental toughness that carried her through the lava bed in better shape than me.

Maybe she just didn't doubt like I did. I never saw her guide, although she said he or maybe she was close by. Tonto was beside me and didn't tap me on the shoulder to warn me away from this lady named Sara who was to be my traveling companion. I wondered why I couldn't see her guide when I was able to see the others earlier. Tonto told me that I was able to see the others to help me understand what consequences bad choices can have.

We found shade and water after the lava field and were able to get back on our way, still a little weak, but moving a little better. Not much further, we came to a steep cliff that we couldn't see either end of and after looking at our guides, guessed we needed to work together to get over it. There was a small ledge about halfway up that if we could make it that far, we could make it the rest of the way. We couldn't find any footholds or handholds so we needed to think of something else. Sara finally came up with the idea to go back to the trees and get a log to climb up to make it to the top of the first ledge. When I asked her if she'd done this kind of thing before, she said she hadn't. I asked her how she came up with the log idea and she said she simply asked her guide. I looked at Tonto and he just smiled and shrugged his shoulders.

The log idea worked and we were able to continue on our way. The sun was getting lower in the sky and it looked like we might make it after all. We were getting hungry by then and started talking about our favorite foods. We hoped that when we got to the lodge that they would feed us like we were told. I couldn't wait! I told her that I wanted the biggest steak they could find. She got real quiet and I sensed that I'd said something that bothered her so

I asked her what her problem was. You know, sometimes I'm just not very tactful and evidently there's a better way of asking that particular question.

"We don't know each other very well yet and I'm not sure that I want to, either!"

"What?"

"You would kill and eat a poor, defenseless animal?"

"I wouldn't kill it, somebody else gets to do that! I'll just eat it because they taste so good!" I thought that was a clever thing to come up with but she didn't.

"Here I thought you were a kind and thoughtful man. Don't you have any compassion at all? You take a poor defenseless creature that God placed here on earth for us to enjoy and you have to destroy it!"

Now my dander was getting up a little. Those "poor defenseless creatures" that I happen to like to eat have nearly killed ME several times.

"Well, at least my food is dead before I eat it!"

"What's that supposed to mean?"

"Do you eat potatoes?"

"Yes ," she said warily. "Why?"

"Did you know that you can take a potato and put it in the ground and it will grow and produce more potatoes?"

"Yes, so what?"

"The simple fact that it doesn't bother you to eat a living thing, while the food I prefer is dead seems a little hypocritical to me. The potato you eat is still alive or it wouldn't grow!" This seemed to be a concept she'd never considered before and thankfully ended the discussion.

The terrain got a little more rough and rocky as we traveled and I seriously wondered if we would make it before the end of the day or not. That's when the wind started. Gently at first, then it came with a vengeance, shrieking like a tormented demon, hurling dust, leaves, twigs and even tree branches all over the place stinging our eyes, scratching and sandblasting our arms and exposed skin. We had to watch out for each other for protection as we traveled to keep from getting seriously injured. We would move from one big rock or tree to another slowly making our way up the remainder of the mountain. We had to cover our mouths and noses with our shirt sleeves so that we could breathe in the thick, dusty air.

It seemed the closer we got to the top, the harder the way became. I looked back at Tonto and he seemed completely unfazed by any of it, as usual. He just smiled and gave an encouraging nod toward the hill in front of us.

"How much further?" I asked him.

"You'll know when you get there ," came the cryptic reply.

"Thanks a lot!"

The sun didn't have much further to go before it brushed the skyline and the wind had calmed down to a breeze. In front of us were others who were still moving forward but were obviously struggling. One man had been injured in the windstorm and was limping slightly, but that wasn't his worst challenge. He was blind.

How he got this far without seeing was a miracle to me! Then it came to me. Every one of us has a guide. Our own guide that others can't see or hear. As long as we listened to our guide, we would be guided toward our goal. It didn't mean that we would be free of challenges or trials, or even injury, but we would make it. With that realization, I looked at Tonto again and he gave me a big encouraging smile as if he could read my thoughts.

"Do you think that if that man had listened to his guide better, he would have avoided blindness or getting hurt? ," I asked Sara.

"It doesn't matter what I think. But since you asked, I'll share my opinion with you. None of us followed the same path or way to get here. Some were similar sure, but we all experienced different challenges on our way here that makes our journey unique to each of us. Some had it a lot harder than others, while some appeared to have it relatively easy. We don't know what internal challenges anyone else is going through because often we can't see any outward signs. I think one of the reasons for trials is so that we can help others through their trials because of our experiences.

"Oh yeah. Sure. Okay."

We joined up with the other travelers and listened to accounts of their journey's while moving along. Some had started out with good friends that, although they promised to stick together all the way up, gave up when the trials or difficulties came. Then they accused those dedicated to the journey of abandoning their friendship and agreement, when in reality the opposite was true. Others like Sara and I had found support from fellow travelers on their own journey. Several had gotten lost in the darkness but had been able to find their way back to their guide, or were helped by others until they and their guide were reunited.

The sun was disappearing from view and none of us could see the lodge but there was a calm feeling about it that we would be fine. We kept going forward as a group, helping and encouraging those who needed help. While the sun was setting, it didn't seem to be getting any darker! At least around our group it was still light. Finally, as we crested a rise, there was the lodge! It was beautiful! The end of our journey was in sight and it seemed to give each of us a little more energy and confidence with each step. It was still quite a distance away, but we knew without question that it was there! The anticipation was palpable as we all moved forward toward our journey's reward. I could already taste that hot, juicy steak! Sara could have her vegetables. I couldn't wait!

There was another low spot to go through on the last stretch . In it sat a huge building that turned out to be another lodge. I could smell the food cooking and there were people sitting around tables on the patio outside eating their meal, obviously enjoying themselves in the cool evening air. The patrons greeted us warmly and invited us to join them for food and lodging. I'll have to admit that the invitation was nearly overpowering due to the fact that I was absolutely famished and close to physical collapse.

"I'm starved!" I looked over to see who made the comment and was shocked to see that Sara was the source.

"So am I!" said someone else.

"I am absolutely beat!"....And so it went.

"Sara, where is your guide? You have followed your guide all this way, don't give up! Come with me and finish your journey! We can make it together. You have given me hope and helped me get this far. Please don't quit now! We both know it's there, not here that we need to be! The goal is within our grasp!" Our grasp? Yes, she encouraged and counseled me when I needed it. We had become a team on the last part of our journey, leaning on one another, relying on each other for strength, both physically and mentally.

"Stop tapping my shoulder! I'm tired and hungry. I just want to stop, rest and eat something!" she snapped...

"Sara, no one I can see is tapping your shoulder."

Surprised, she looked around seeing only me close by.

"Let's go. We can make it together."

We watched as several in our group joined the others at the tables. The food smelled so good that it almost spoke to us and the thought of resting in a soft bed that night was almost overpowering. The soft glow of the dining lights only added to the already attractive ambiance. Is the other lodge, the one we've been traveling to, as attractive and rewarding as this? Right now, it was almost impossible to imagine anything even close to this, let alone better. This was as good a reward as most could hope for, so they settled for what we'd been told was less. at least we that remained, hoped the extra faith and effort would pay off. As our now smaller group turned to leave, some looked back, gave in and left us.

I took Sara's hand and we put our backs to the great smell of food and immediate rest and comfort, hoping for better, although wondering how that could possibly be.

The blind man led the way. Although he couldn't see, he seemed to have the best vision for this tiny group of straggling travelers. It was nearly dark when we crested the final hill of our journey. There before us sat the most glorious site my eyes have ever beheld. The Lodge looked beautiful from afar but now that we were nearly to it, it was indescribable. It seemed to be it's own light, illuminating the entire mountain top with a beautiful warm, inviting glow. Even more than the place we left earlier. The light was a more pure light. That sounds confusing, but it was a clean, pure illumination that left no shadows anywhere. It also had a different feel to it. Where the other lodge was warm and friendly, this place felt familiar, it was like we belonged here. It felt like we were coming home.

Suddenly, we saw what appeared to be horses and wagons coming out to meet us. It was the welcoming committee. As they got closer, I realized that they weren't wagons at all, they were chariots pulled by horses so swift they didn't seem to touch the ground. We watched as they literally glided toward us, mesmerized by the seemingly magical spectacle. The powerful horses were gentle, yet majestic. The chariots were gorgeous and comfortable with shining pure white bodies and lots of gold trim on the edges and wheels. The drivers seemed to be surprisingly grateful that we made it and were very kind and helpful. As we neared the Lodge, we could hear beautiful, soft music emanating from somewhere inside and for a moment we forgot our hunger and fatigue. It truly was indescribable and we hadn't eaten a bite yet!

We were taken inside the building where we were given a soothing cool drink and toasted bread of some sort before being escorted to our rooms where we were able to get cleaned up and put on clean clothes. We were never hurried, but the staff was efficient while never acting like they were hurrying. We were allowed to comfortably set our own pace without feeling rushed.

As we entered the dining hall, we were greeted by name and escorted to our tables. "How do they know who I am? ," I wondered. I was glad to join up with Sara again and was curious as to what was on the menu!

"Were you greeted by your name?" I asked Sara.

"Of course ," she said.

As I asked the question, I had to do a double-take. Sara had changed! Not just her clothes, but after cleaning up, she was beautiful! She had an aura around her that made her glow. Her appearance wasn't that different, but the glow she had was stunning! She truly was a Lady in every respect.

While looking around the room, I recognized others whom we had met on our journey. The blind man with the limp wasn't limping any more and he appeared to be able to see! Those who had helped him were present, but I couldn't find Tonto.

"Is your guide here, Sara?"

"No, all the guides left after we got here. They have others to help."

"How can anyone go through what we just went through and have the strength and energy to do it all over again so soon? It's the end of the day! Nobody will start up the trail in the dark! Do they have a secret way down to the trailhead? Is there a road we don't know about? They must've gone to bed to rest up. Yeah, they had to have done that. What about your guide? Tonto never seemed affected by anything we did, like he was super human or something.

Sara just looked at me with a touch of sadness, or maybe compassion in her eyes. "You don't get it, do you?"

Get what? Why do you always seem to have all the answers while I'm always in the dark? The only time I know of that you even came close to wavering was back at the other lodge."

"Yes, thanks to you I made it. WE made it!" She gave me a smile that penetrated my very soul. I suddenly realized how much we had relied on each other and the challenges we'd overcome together. I was getting to be very fond of this Lady.

"Was it only one day that this journey had lasted? It now seems much longer."

"The journey isn't over, yet."

"What! There's more?" The thought of going any further after today was devastating and completely disheartening.

"We haven't eaten yet!" she said with a smile. "That's the culmination and reward of the journey!"

"Oh yeah. Food. I am hungry!"

No sooner than the words left my lips than a waiter appeared with our appetizers. We hadn't ordered anything yet, but here came our favorite appetizers! Jalapeno poppers for me and cabbage rolls for Sara. I'll stick with the poppers. The sight brought my hunger up to a ravenous level! I was about to do a serious attack on them when I noticed Sara's head lowered in prayer. Ashamed at my own selfishness, I dropped my head and gave heartfelt thanks for the day, but especially for the food!

"May I have your attention for a moment?"

The voice was powerful, yet soft and gentle. The question or announcement really, brought us out our efforts to make our appetizers disappear. "I would like to thank all of you who made the journey to The Lodge today. We are so grateful and pleased you made it. I know it took a huge degree of dedication and even sacrifice for each of you to make it. You needed to listen to and heed the counsel your guides offered in order to be here. You helped each other and were willing to leave your self-centered desires behind. All of you overcame physical, mental and spiritual challenges to be able to rest here tonight. Out of the many who began the journey, you are the few who persevered and displayed the courage as well as the obedience and fortitude to enjoy this reward. Doubt, discouragement, ridicule and deception were your constant antagonists. Some whom you thought were loyal friends were left behind. It took vision, faith, and unselfish teamwork to accomplish this goal. Those who dropped out were those that lost the vision, faith and unselfishness, or never had it in the first place.

"Let me replay the journey for you. I will compare your journey to your life. You started out with no real idea what lie before you, but you had faith and hope that something good or even great could be accomplished if you continued on the way your guide directed. None of you knew at that point exactly what the reward would be. Most of you still don't, that's why I'm explaining this to you.

"In the beginning, you encountered the snags and every day stumbling blocks of life represented by the brush you had to go through. The triumph of overcoming failure and these obstacles gave you hope and confidence to continue on and made the next so-called insurmountable obstacle less formidable. Each small victory added a little more confidence and faith to your weapons bag, so to speak.

"Next came darkness and uncertainty. You had to stay close to your guide to make it through the canyon of darkness. Though there were many there who invited you to share their meager light, you continued on looking for a greater light. You weren't lured onto dark paths that only took you further into the darkness to be lost. Some of you stepped off the path only to discover that it wasn't where you needed to go."

I thought of Randy and how close I came to leaving the path. If it wasn't for Tonto, I'd have been lost too.

"After struggling up the mountain you came to a beautiful, cool green area with refreshing water and rest. Many people stayed there, afraid of the ridicule from others who hadn't the faith to continue on."

I thought of the young woman there who turned from what I thought was a friendly, beautiful lady into a controlling, narcissistic fiend.

"Then came the furnace of affliction or, in other words, the lava rocks. Many more people turned back after finding it was too much for them, but you didn't! Those who turned back to tell of what they found led many people astray, as you saw. This was where your silver was purged. This was where you were seriously tested. This was where your journey took on more meaning. All of you formed friendships there that strengthened your resolve to finish your course. These friendships will be and are eternal. From that point forward you worked together to overcome the temptations and trials that you faced. It is supposed to be this way. We weren't meant to journey alone!"

I looked over at Sara and saw her looking at me. Her eyes smiled at me and I smiled back.

"Another challenge came in the form of the windstorm. You kept going forward. You didn't stop. You didn't quit! Even when you were getting whipped and beaten by everything coming at you, breathing was a challenge and you couldn't see where you were going, sand and debris scoured your exposed skin and blinded your way, you didn't give up!

"The Adversary will let you accomplish some spiritual goals only to hit you with everything he has just to make you fail. Then he laughs at your supposed failures. The shrieking, buffeting wind shows his anger and frustration at you for not giving in to his will.

"The Imposter Lodge was next. You were tired and hungry and the people there encouraged you to stay. The food smelled heavenly, the atmosphere was inviting, the thought of rest and food was nearly overpowering. But you continued on, some with encouragement from friends."

I could feel Sara's eyes on me so I looked up into her face. She had a look that was pure gratitude, with a trace of a tear in her eyes. I liked Sara. I really liked Sara. I really liked Sara a lot!

"With the exception of Brother Johnson, all of you had seen The Lodge before you got to the other one. You finally knew it existed and was on your way. A little more sacrifice and the goal is in sight. Your faith in something you had never been to, or up to now, never really knew existed, is now being rewarded. Those that chose to stop early will never have any idea what they are missing by settling for a lesser existence.

"You may have noticed that your guides seemed familiar to you. They should, they are family members or friends who have left the earthly life and are now your guardian angels. They aren't burdened with pain or physical suffering like you. They aren't bound by the earth or it's laws. Even when you can't see them any more, they are there watching over you. trying to protect you from evil and danger. As long as you are trying to follow the teachings of the Savior, They will be there for you. Enjoy your meal and your stay. Welcome home!"

With that, our food was set out in front of us. It looked and smelled fantastic! My steak was sizzling and the baked potato was steaming with a big serving of butter and sour cream next to it. Sara had a plate full of alfalfa sprouts with some asparagus covered in a sauce of some sort and a small plate with sliced fruit and a fruit smoothie! I have to admit, it did look pretty good, but I'm starved out so almost anything looks good right now!

"Would you care for a bite of this delicious protein before I devour it?"

"Only if you take a small bite of this asparagus!"

Wow! I didn't expect that! The asparagus was actually good, but I was looking forward to her eating some meat. I cut a small piece off for her and she looked into my eyes and opened her mouth for the bite. I watched as the bite passed between those beautiful lips and then I woke up. WAIT!…WHAT!!... I WOKE UP!!.. Noooo!!.. No steak?...No Potato? No SARA!! OOOHHHH!!

Dreams can be so cruel!

The Apostle Paul talked about the three degrees of glory in his first letter to the Corinthians. The first rest spot with the green grass and cool water represents the Telestial Kingdom or the glory of the stars where most people will end up after death. People who lie, cheat, murder and are immoral will be here. It's a degree of glory, but it's not where God the Father dwells. The Imposter Lodge represents the Terrestial kingdom or the glory of the moon. This is where, like the story indicates, honorable men that lost the true vision of Jesus Christ will be. Those who received His gospel, but didn't live up to it. They were willing to settle for less than the best. The Lodge represents the Celestial Kingdom or the glory of the sun and all it's glory. This is where God the Father dwells and all who are valiant in serving Jesus Christ and following His ordinances will be there too.

CHAPTER 4

Jack's Place

Since a lot of the stories in here took place at the Jack Brewer place, I guess I'll try to put together some of the more memorable ones in one place. This looks like a good place to start.

The first trip I made to Jack's started at the Wolf Den. That was the winter camp and now that it was May, it was time to start the move to Jack's to get ready for the spring branding.

Gary Broome and I needed to trail the horse herd from the Wolf Den to Jack's. I'd never been there and Gary told me that it was about a 15 mile ride one way. We'd be dropping the horses off there and riding back the same day. Trailing horses is fun because you're not just walking and dawdling along, you're generally moving at a trot or a lope the whole way.

We headed down Brewer Canyon and were a mile or so from the mouth where it hits Bitter creek when Gary decided it was time to get out in front so he could turn them up the creek toward Jack's. He was riding a four year old sorrel gelding ranch horse he called Quaker. Gary had been riding him all winter and Quaker was coming along pretty well.

There was a black horse in the bunch that had been owned by a guy named Jim before the ranch bought him. The horse was called "Nigger Jim". As Gary started to get around the horses, they picked up speed a little. He had to kick Quaker up a notch to get him around them and as he passed Jim, the horse kicked Gary's left leg pretty hard.

"My leg's broke! He broke my leg!" he exclaimed.

We were a long way from where we needed to be and I had no idea where that was. I was riding a horse that belonged to Gary's mom named Q Ball. He was short and stout and had some pretty good speed. I was able to get around the horses and head them up the creek.

"If you can tell me where to go and what to do, I'll try to get the horses up there," I told him. He said that he could make it so off we went.

He had grit, I'll hand him that! The rest of the trip was uneventful until we were about a mile from Brewer canyon on the way back.

"Layne, I've got to pee".

"Well, get off and pee!"

"I can't"

"Why not?"

"I can't get off this horse"

"Can't you get off the offside?"

"No, he won't let me."

We rode on a little further and again we went through the same routine.

"I've REALLY got to go!"

"Well, if you can't get off, then you're going to have to do it from your saddle".

He ended up undoing his chaps and leaned over as far as he could, then dribbled down his chaps. This taught me a very important lesson while working with horses. Work on and off both sides so that if you have to get off the off side, there won't be a problem or a question. His leg wasn't broken after all, but it was pretty sore for a while. Jim had worn out his welcome and, as Jon was loading him up in the trailer for the last time, Jim tried to kick Jon too. He went away and we never saw him again.

....

We probably spent more time there than anywhere due to the fact that it was used in the spring as a gathering place to brand the new calves on their way to the mountain and in the fall to gather the cows and to wean the calves. By the first of July, we were usually comfortably settled up on the mountain. It never seemed like the warm, easy summers lasted long enough. Before we knew it, it was late fall again and time to move camp back to Jack's place. That's where we would wean the calves before trailing them the three days from the corrals at Jack's up Augussi Canyon and down Dragon Canyon to the remains of Dragon City on Evacuation Creek, up Missouri Creek then over Park Canyon ridge into the Park.

....

That trail ride was in late December and I can remember dropping the calves in Dragon Canyon after dark and trotting our horses down the trail and seeing the sparks come off Gary Broome's horse's shod hooves when they struck a rock. I also remember being cold. Once, when we were walking our horses down the trail after dropping the calves off, I was pretty cold and nobody was talking. We were all cold, it being well below zero, so I got off my horse and started walking to warm up a little. It didn't take long for the others to do the same!

....

In the Spring, we would get up around 4:30 am, wrangle the horses, fix and eat breakfast on the coal stove, saddle our horses and be on our way for the 12-15 mile ride to get to the cows before the sun came up and the cows shaded up. The horse wrangler was usually the youngest cowboy and he would ride old Red bareback in the dark. Red would hit a nice, easy lope, find the horses and bring them back to the corral.

All the wrangler had to do was to hang on and not fall off. The horses knew the routine so we never had any trouble that I can remember. We would gather all the cows and calves we could find and head them down to Bitter creek, then up through the swamp. We'd leave them there to rest up while we went to Jack's to eat a lunch of bread with canned deviled ham and butter and then take a nap until about 4:00 when we'd saddle another horse and go down the creek then bring them all up to the branding corrals to brand the next morning.

The first branding of the season was usually the hardest. I remember branding 40 or so calves once and being completely beat. A couple days later, we branded over 80 and never even got tired! There were about five of us for the spring branding. Bill Slaugh was only 14 and unbeknownst to us, was terrified of snakes. Since he was the youngest, he was elected to be the horse wrangler.

We must have gathered the cows the day before because he was wrangling in the daylight when he came blowing into the cabin just beside himself. After he calmed down, he said he'd seen a snake. I'd never seen anyone so terrified of anything as he was of that snake! Nobody ever cried about anything. I guess that's what surprised us and made us all take notice. If we made any audible exclamation at all, it was usually either a muffled grunt or a loud single syllable curse word expressed with an impressive amount of gusto and feeling! Crying just wasn't done.

....

Sometimes we would use the mid-day rest to fix broken tack or school our horses. I owned a horse that would nearly jerk your arm off if you shot around him while holding the reins so I thought it would do him some good to put some hobbles on him to get him to stay put while shooting my pistol.

I found out that he could run almost as fast with hobbles on as he could without them! I walked down into the pasture to catch him and was in the middle of the horse herd when I saw a crippled up coyote about 50 yards away. He hadn't seen me yet, so I pulled my pistol out and waited until he showed up between two horses and then I shot him. We'd lost several new calves up to that point, but after that, we didn't lose any more. Also, I got to walk a mile back to the corral because none of the other horses liked being shot around either!

I had to think of something better. I came up with another scathingly brilliant idea. I'd hobble him, but tied my lariat around the hobbles and then tied the other end to a solid post. Well, this time he didn't make it very far before his tail end went flying over his head and he ended up flat on the ground wondering what happened! After that, whenever I put hobbles on him, he wouldn't move his front feet at all.

....

Gary Broome and I had been at Jack's for a while getting ready to move to the Wolf Den camp in a couple weeks. We'd been eating elk meat for what seemed like forever and I wanted something different. We got an inch or two of snow when I told him that I was going to see if I could find a rabbit.

I strapped on my pistol and went hunting. I ended up with two of the plump little rodents and went back to camp to cook 'em up. They ended up being the best meat I'd had in quite a while! Normally, I'm not that big a fan of rabbit meat, but I really wanted a change and as good as elk meat is, the change was great!

....

I was riding a two year old buckskin filly that I was buying from the ranch and she was coming along really well. We were gathering cows and calves in the afternoon out of the upper end of the swamp below the horse pasture for the next days branding. I named her Sage and was starting to really like her.

The neighbor, Shorty Hatch, had an old crippled up black bull there that we all called "Shorty". Anyway, we were just about out of the swamp and Sage and I were in the back waiting for the cows to move on out, when here comes Shorty. He couldn't move very fast but he must have made Sage nervous because as I was turned in the saddle with my right hand resting on her rump, she jumped out from under me! I landed headfirst in the swamp with my fairly new hat. That hat had a tough spring! It got baptized in the swamp then got tattooed by a deer later on. Shorty didn't get me and

Sage didn't run off too far so no harm was done. The other guys got a good chuckle out of it, though!

....

Weaning the calves was kind of fun. We would gather a bunch of cows and calves in the corral, then split the calves from the cows and take the cows down the creek a couple miles and shut the gate behind them so they couldn't come back. We would have to get them to go as fast as we could ..usually at a run...so they wouldn't know their calves weren't with them until after they got through the lower gate a mile and a half later. The calves had water and feed and after a few days they would stop bawling for their moms and start eating. We would gather all we could find until we thought we had all or most of them. The cows and their calves would usually come down the mountain on their own and would be waiting at the gate to come on through.

One of the rules of cow camp was not to complain about the cooking. The penalty was two weeks of dish washing. Bitter Creek runs through the wrangle pasture that's right next to the house but we used water from the cistern that caught all the water and snow- melt that came off the roof. This spring Wade was the wrangler and Gary Broome was the cook. Wade headed out to gather the horses and Gary was going to whip up some pancakes for breakfast. We had some really tough fibrous towels that weren't quite paper but must have had some cloth fibers mixed in them. They were tough. I asked Gary if he wanted to play a trick on Wade. He always liked tricks...as long as they weren't on him! We took a coffee can and used it for a pattern and Gary made a beautiful pancake with one of the towels inside. Wade always had a pretty healthy appetite so it was going to be fun to watch how he reacted to this. Wade is also pretty wise to trickery himself and quickly figured out just what was up. He scraped the pancake crumbs off the towel and piled them up on the side of his plate. When Gary asked him if anything was wrong, Wade insisted that everything was just fine! When asked about the pile of crumbs on the side of his plate, he explained, "I eat them this way all the time!"

We all got a good laugh out of it!

....

One horse in my string of three was a big, stout black horse that came out of the wild bunch from Douglas Mountain by the Yampa River. He was owned by Donny Moore who was the veterinarian that did a lot of the work for the Ranch. Donny grew up in Rangely and was a good friend. Donny left Blackbird, as he was called, for us to ride. Blackbird was a horse you had better respect or bad things could happen in a hurry! I was told that he'd buck me off if I wasn't careful. I liked him even if he was pretty spooky and even kind of waspy. No one had ever tried to rope off him because of that. He could really travel and had a walk that most horses had a hard time keeping up with. I told the guys that I would rope calves off him and they just kind of raised their eyebrows at that. Something to look forward to seeing!

Like I said, he was tough and I rode him several 40 mile days in a row before I took my rope down on him. I was able to kind of control him and keep him from running away! After a while he was dragging bushes that I'd roped behind him and I figured it was time to rope some calves.

That morning came soon enough and it came my turn to rope. I tightened up my cinch, stepped on him and rode him around a couple circles before I got my rope down as all eyes watched in anticipation. No trouble...yet. I screwed myself down into my saddle the best I could. I threw my first loop and roped the first of many calves we'd catch that spring. He was a little nervous but I think he trusted me enough to listen to me. He just got better and better after that. He never did try to buck with me, and I'm glad because he was solid and really stout! By the time Donny came out later that summer, Blackbird was handling like a dream. Donny was really happy with him and gave me some pretty generous compliments on my horsemanship.

We usually only had two changes of clothes all the time we were there. We would wear one set all the time we were working and the other set was for going back to civilization. It got so that the one set would nearly rear up and fight you by the time we went to town! We would wash our faces and hands in the basin but the rest of our person smelled like horse sweat, our sweat, processed second hand cattle feed and branding smoke. We were so used to it that it didn't bother us and we didn't notice it. We'd knock the outer layer of accumulated grime off and put the clean clothes on before we left. Most of the time anyway. I remember once when I didn't have or take time to clean up before going home. My mom barely let me in the house to clean up! At first, she wasn't even sure who I was!

We would rope the calves any way we could unless they were bigger, then we would catch them by the head and heels. Wade was a stout young man often looking for ways to test his strength. One time there was an extra large calf and Wade told whoever was roping to catch it by the head and he'd throw it down and tie it.

Well, it turned into a pretty interesting wrestling match to say the least! Sometimes Wade was on top, then the calf would be on top. This went on for a while until Wade finally prevailed, but not without some collateral damage to his seasoned pants. During the contest of wills, the calf kicked Wade inside his upper thigh effectively ripping the seams down both pant legs until he nearly had a fancy skirt on!

The bottoms were still intact around his boots, but that was all. We were pretty isolated and were a long way from any civilization, but sometimes we'd get some company. Usually in the form of bear hunters. Well, just after Wades blowout, Shirley Cook came by to visit. It was fun to watch Wade standing at attention with his knees stuck together, legs straight and not moving! I think he must've had another pair of pants back at the cabin, but he finished out the rest of the branding that day in his breezy britches!

CHAPTER 5

Chipita Deer Hunt

While working on the Cripple Cowboy, we sometimes ran a little short on groceries at the spring cow camp. We were at the old Jack Brewer place on Bitter creek. Jack's Place, as it was called, was a solid log cabin with a wood/coal burning stove that we did all our cooking on. There were a couple more buildings in addition to the necessary outhouse.

One morning, as we were getting ready to saddle our horses and gather cows and calves for branding, I was occupying said outhouse. It was still dark and I could hear footsteps coming my way. When the door opened, I said something like, "You're not sitting on MY lap!"

It was Gary Broome and he jumped back and quickly shut the door! I finished up and caught and saddled my horse. I don't think he tried it again that morning. Scared him pretty good!

This particular time we were down to sugar, flour, and some rice. We were out of meat. It was June and the deer were growing antlers so it wouldn't be hard to tell the difference between a doe and a buck. It was decided that we would go to Chipita Canyon to find our sustenance for the next couple weeks. Gary had the only rifle so he would be the shooter. He also had the only truck so he'd be the driver too. Chipita was about seven miles away so Wade and I bailed into the truck with Gary and headed that way that evening.

We'd only gone a little way up the canyon when a young buck walked out in front of us. Gary stopped the truck, grabbed his rifle and bailed out pretty quickly. The buck was standing broadside only about 50 yards away and Gary had a good rest across the hood of his truck. Wade and I stayed in the truck and stayed still so Gary would have a steady shot. He fired a shot and the deer moved a little way off. Gary missed him altogether! At the sound of the second shot, the buck humped up and ran off to lay under some oak brush about 125 yards away.

"You gut shot him," I said.

We got out of the truck as Gary and his dog Yogi walked up to the suffering deer. We watched as he just stood next to it and I hollered to him to finish it off.

About this time, Wade and I started to walk that direction and I remember telling Wade to be careful in case the deer got up because Gary wasn't a very good shot. We were in some tall sagebrush when the deer got tired of being stared at and got up and took off. Guess where? Yup, right toward Wade and me.

There was a big sagebrush that was about seven or eight feet high that we were hiding behind, but it didn't even slow the deer down. By this time I was more concerned...worried, really...about the possibility/probability of getting shot than I was worried about the deer hurting us. But it kept coming right toward us when finally, we had to literally jump out of the way! Wade jumped one direction and I jumped the wrong direction. I was still in the air parallel with the ground when we first met. Now I'd had quite a few meetings with deer in my life up to this point, but none like this one! Like I said, I was still airborne when that deer hit me.

I was wearing a fairly new, in decent shape, hat. Until then, anyway. That buck did a quick tap dance on my hat, on my back and various other parts of my anatomy before he continued on his way. I stayed low, not because I was hurt, but because I knew Gary was possibly pointing his gun in my direction. Safety first, you know!

Well, Yogi ended up being the hero when he cornered the buck long enough for Gary to finish it off. We ended up having enough to eat until it was time to go to the mountain camp for the summer.

CHAPTER 6

Rooster

Rooster was young a ranch horse that ended up in my riding string for the fall. He was a sorrel colored horse around 1050 pounds and he was tough. I liked him quite a bit most of the time. Gary Smith and I were kicking the cattle off the mountain into the lower country for the coming winter and Rooster was my horse for the day.

One calf (*there's always at least one!*) was trying to get away. "Shucks, I'll just have to rope the errant little beast!"

So I did, just as he hit the edge of some spruce trees and quakies. I dallied up and turned Rooster around so we could pull the calf out where he needed to go when Rooster bogged his head and tried to buck! He found out that it was pretty tough to accomplish this with a 400 pound drag keeping his feet on the ground! We got the job done and lived happily to fight another day.

Later that winter, I must have been either at the Wolf Den cow camp or still at Jack's place, but Jon wanted me to ride to the mountain from Jack's and check for stragglers that hadn't made it down to the lower country. Anyway, I left from Jack's and rode up Rat Hole Canyon up over the top and back down into Bitter Creek where the summer camp was at. It was a long 14 miles with the snow up to Rooster's belly on top of the mountain.

It had just snowed a couple days before so any tracks I found would be fresh. We went to all the likely spots I thought cows might be and never saw any sign so the third day we headed back toward Jack's place by following the ridge that runs on the south of Bitter Creek. As we got to the top forks of Chipita Canyon, we headed down into the canyon itself. It got pretty steep and the snow was still a couple feet deep at one point so I tied the reins up on the saddle and broke trail down to the bottom of the canyon with Rooster following along behind. We made it to Jack's without any trouble and without any cattle either.

The following summer I was in Chipita Canyon and thought I'd try to see where we came off into the canyon the previous winter. I was shaken as I realized that we had come down a bald expanse of sandstone. Not really a cliff, but not far from it. How we made it off that steep rock without starting an avalanche and killing ourselves was shocking. Again, I attribute it to guardian angels and a mother's prayers for a son that evidently had a habit of making less than smart decisions!

CHAPTER 7

Quaker and the Sheep

Gary Broome and I were at the Park and, for reasons I can't remember, rode our horses down Park Canyon where it ends at Evacuation Creek. It was early spring time and the sheep were on the north side of the fence where they were supposed to be. Yogi, Gary's dog was with us. Gary told me to watch him as he didn't like sheep and might try to hurt one if he got a chance. Sure enough, about half way down the canyon, we realized Yogi was missing. We looked around and saw him across the fence with a sheep. Gary got him back, scolded him and we continued on our way.

We got to the end of the canyon and rode up Evacuation Creek a little ways to check on things. There were some sheep on our side of the fence. Gary hadn't ever had anything to do with sheep before and asked me what to do. I told him that we could just herd them like cows and push them through the gate by the road. He expressed his complete disdain of sheep and was glad that there wasn't anyone around to see him herding these stupid sheep. It could ruin his reputation for life!

He was riding a green horse named Quaker that probably hadn't ever seen a sheep up until then. In order to get them through the gate, they had to go over a small hill then make a sharp turn to the road and gate. Gary and Quaker were on the other side of the hill, or hump really. I was to bring them to him and he was to turn them toward the road and through the gate.

Well, I didn't have any trouble getting around them and heading them to the hump. They took off running away from me and as they came over the hill toward Quaker, he was completely convinced that the scary, wooly horde boiling over the hill was coming to take him to the deepest, darkest abyss of Gehenna! Since he didn't want that to happen, he decided to outrun them...and he did! Gary was pulling on the reins and hollering in frustration and anger while Quaker was running for his life! Fortunately, I was able to keep from falling off my horse while laughing at the terror stricken pair!

The sheep saw their victims making big circles out through the brush at a high rate of speed and slowed down enough to watch so I was able to get around them and through the gate without any more potential bloodshed or fright.

We were headed back up the canyon when we noticed Yogi was missing again. Gary wheeled Quaker back and headed back through the gate. Yogi hadn't committed any crimes as yet and as Gary was closing the gate, a pickup came by and stopped to tell Gary that there were more of his sheep down the road a little further. Gary let him know that the sheep did NOT belong to him and caught back up to me in a huff. I heard the conversation, so I thought I'd have a little fun with it.

"Well?"

"Well what?"

"Well… are you going to take care of your other sheep, or not?!"

We just about had a horse race!

CHAPTER 8

Guardian Angels

We all do foolish things on our walk through life. At times, it seems as though we are protected from our actions by a higher power. Other times, we are left to learn from the unwise decisions we make. As time was close for me to leave for my mission, I asked our stake patriarch, Elmer Bair, for a blessing. I was told some pretty interesting things about myself, but one thing that caught my attention was when I was told that I had kept my guardian angels busy. I noticed that he said angels, not angel. It made me wonder what he was talking about, so I started to think about some of the experiences I'd had that may have fit in that category. I surprised myself with more than I had expected. Here are some that came to mind:

Spring Break

It was my second semester at Ricks College and time for Spring Break. I was anxious to go home and see my parents and the Ranch. My roommate, Scott, was from a Chicago suburb and wouldn't be able to go home so I invited him to come along. He gladly accepted.

I wanted to show him around the area a little so one of the things we decided to do was to take the Jeep across the river and down to Cowboy Canyon. It was a beautiful, warm, sunny spring day. We had a good time and got a flat tire on the way back. The jack wouldn't go high enough so I got hold of the back end and lifted the jeep high enough for Scott to slide a couple rocks under it to get the job done. He was impressed, but Jeeps aren't that heavy for a young man in decent shape.

When we got back to the river where we needed to cross, there was a little water flowing over the top of the ice where we had crossed earlier that day. I put the jeep in four wheel drive and told Scott to keep his door open. We eased out onto the ice, then I floor-boarded it. We got almost all the way across before the back wheels fell through, but we were going fast enough that the front wheels pulled us on across. We caught a little air when we hit the bank on the other side! Not the smartest thing I've ever done.

Horses

This next section deals with some experiences involving horses, obviously. These aren't in chronological order, but they still happened.

Wild Horse Scheme

There was a wild mare hanging around the area. I'd spent some time with my brother in Texas and happened to bring back a yearling colt that I'd picked up fairly cheap. I got this great idea of starting our own wild horse herd close to home and thought these two would get along pretty well together. I was going to need some help for this to all come together so I called Wade. He was always up for adventure and hadn't learned yet that not all of my schemes were good ideas. Good times maybe, but not always good ideas.

I gathered up the mare and in a couple days she'd kind of lead and follow another horse. I had two horses I could ride, Skeets and Sage. Skeets was a gelding and a really good saddle horse. Sage was a mare and gentle. She was also in heat, which isn't good when there's a stud around. I rode Skeets and led the colt while Wade got to lead the mare on Sage. We got about halfway across the river when the mare bolted and got away from Wade. She took off up the river (*like she wasn't supposed to do*) with Wade in hot pursuit. I had to find a strong limb to tie the colt up to before I could help out so it took a while. I finally caught up to them about three-quarters of a mile later. Wade had gotten around her and headed her back the way she'd just come from. I saw them coming and had my rope down. I planned on roping her as soon as I could. Here's where the angels came in. I say angels because I'm convinced that there were good ones and bad ones.

I came up on the wild mare pretty quick and threw the prettiest loop I've ever thrown in my life. I watched as it floated over her head and dropped in just perfectly. Problem was the trail had narrowed down to an eyebrow on a mighty steep hillside. It wasn't a cliff, but not far from it. Just as the loop dropped down, Skeets stepped on her lead rope and popped my rope off. Thankfully! She fell down and knocked Skeets down, too. I got off to help straighten things out and they both got up and took off. My feet got tangled up in the rope and I was bouncing along behind them when Skeets knocked her off the trail. It was probably about 50 feet to the bottom and that's where she ended up. Meanwhile I'd gotten loose from the rope and Skeets had stopped. I'm pretty sure the mare got a concussion out of that deal because her eyes weren't pointed in the same direction at the same time. She didn't give us any more trouble after that.

We didn't end up with our horse herd. The colt came back home and ended up being another really good saddle horse. After riding him for a few years I sold him to a ten year old girl from Craig, Colorado, and she qualified on him for nationals in barrel racing.

Calico

When I was about 14 years old, my dad got into the cow business. That was exciting for me and I looked forward to being a cowboy. Problem was we didn't have a horse. Everybody knows that you're not a cowboy if you don't have a horse to ride. Lorraine Brady sold us an Appaloosa mare named Ginger. She had a colt with her they called Calico. Ginger was a good gentle mare and she taught me a lot about cows. When Calico was big enough to ride, there wasn't anyone to break him so I just started riding him. I didn't know any more than he did so things were interesting at times. His conformation left a lot to be desired. His head and neck were massive. His rear end was barely there. He was hard headed (*I may have had something to do with that*) and couldn't or wouldn't run fast enough to kick up dust in August…really slow.

I went to work for Bob Hilkey at Adams Lodge on Marvine Creek up above Meeker, Colorado, in 1979. Calico was home eating for free and not contributing to anything constructive. Hunting season was coming up and Bob asked if I would be willing to bring that horse up for a while to help out. I thought it was a great idea and went and got him.

Bob used Morgan horses and was pretty proud of them. They were some of the best around. They had good feet and strong bones as well as being excellent trail horses. He didn't have much use for Quarter horses or Appaloosas because their feet and bones, as a rule, weren't big enough to hold their weight. I had ridden Molly as a three year old all summer and really liked her. Her mother was a Percheron mare and her dad was Bob's Morgan stud. One day they got loose from the corral. Molly and Calico were heading for town and I was on foot trying to get around them. I wasn't very fast (and I'm a lot slower now) and was able to get past Molly but couldn't catch up to Calico until Bob came up in his truck.

We gathered them both and shut them up in the corral when Bob said something about Appy's not being able to run very fast. I reminded him that I was able to outrun Molly, but not Calico! He said that she wasn't trying very hard. She wasn't, but it was still fun to razz him about it!

The first time I took Calico up the trail to the Lake Camp was interesting. At home, I'd ridden him across the river and didn't think much about it, but the first little muddy trickle we came to on the trail scared him to death! I couldn't get the stupid thing to cross that three foot wide muddy spot for anything! I rode him the mile back to the corral and got some bailing wire and made a quirt out of it. He still wouldn't go across so I ended up driving the six miles back to the lodge and getting another horse. Bob asked me what took so long after I finally made it to camp and I told him what had happened. The next day we tied Calico to the back of a pack horse and he was dragged across all those little muddy spots all the way to the Lake Camp! He didn't give me any trouble after that.

I ended up working for Jon Hill on his Cripple Cowboy Cow Outfit. (There are many good reasons for that name!) Anyway, I was riding along Bitter Creek just above the branding corrals by the Jack Brewer place when we hit a slick spot and Calico fell before I could kick loose. He landed on his right side pinning my leg under him. My head was a few feet away from the creek and I was afraid we were going to slide off into it. Calico just laid there. He wouldn't get up or even try. I couldn't reach my latigo to take the saddle off. I was stuck under this stupid horse. I spurred him, hollered at him, even shot my pistol next to his ear. He wasn't going to get up. I don't know how long we were there, but after a while I saw this cowboy hat sticking up over the bank. Jon popped his head over and saw us "relaxing" and asked what I was doing down there! He came down and got the saddle off and the horse up without me getting stepped on. I'm pretty sure Jon was inspired to find me, whether he knew it or not.

Another time I was riding Calico, we were loping along and he decided that this was a race he had a chance of winning! Everyone else was at a nice easy lope and he was going about as hard as he could. He was winning! I couldn't get him to slow down and ended up running the stupid thing into a cedar tree on purpose to get him shut down. It slowed him down, but didn't stop him, so we hit another!

He did have a good point or two, though. He was gentle. We were gathering Boulevard Ridge one day and it's a long way from where we needed to go. There was a young calf that just wasn't going to make it so we loaded it up in the saddle with me. Calico couldn't have cared less. The momma cow stayed right next to us all the way to Jack's place several miles away. I traded him to a sheep herder after that.

Psycho Filly

The horses on the Cripple Cowboy were registered quarter horses with racing bloodlines and raised on the ranch. It was summer, and time to sack out the two year olds in preparation to start saddle work and riding. Gary Broome was the horse breaker and he was starting to work with a pretty waspy filly. She wasn't at all happy with what was going on and was letting Gary know it. I was sitting on the top corral pole watching. Gary had a floppy saddle blanket and instead of standing to the side, he was standing right in front of her. As he raised the blanket to her nose, she reared up and slapped him with one of her front feet, knocking him to the ground. I bailed off the fence and tried to stabilize his head for fear that his neck might be broken or injured. Bob, his dad was there and quickly came along with everyone else. Some blood was coming out of Gary's mouth and it was a struggle trying to hold his head still. Finally he jerked free and spit out a mouthful of blood and said something about me trying to drown him! Bob loaded him up and hauled him to Grand Junction to the doctor. He ended up with some loose teeth for a while is all. If she'd of hit him anywhere but the head, she would have hurt him!

It was decided that the filly didn't like men so Jon hauled her to a gal to be trained. After a couple months or more, I got elected to go to the rodeo grounds and pick up the filly. I was driving a one ton ranch truck with stock racks and had to back up to a dirt bank so I could load her up. I found her in a stall and, remembering how fond she was of men, I carefully haltered her, all that time caution bells were going off in my mind. Then I headed for the truck with her in tow. We were almost to the truck when she started acting up. The hair on the back of my neck stood up and I got the distinct impression that someone had stood between us protecting me. I got her home and put her in a small pen without any more trouble. The next morning, Jon and Gary went out to check on her and she came at them with her mouth wide open and teeth bared trying to get them. Nobody tried to ride her after that.

Duke

While I was working at the Cripple Cowboy, I traded for a tall, rangy sorrel horse I ended up naming Duke. He wasn't pretty, but he could really walk and he handled really well too. Plus, it helped that he was in my price range. I was trading the horse I'd gotten from the sheep man in the Calico trade. I planned on using him on the Ranch pushing cows and branding so I asked the trader if this horse had been roped from. I was told that he had, so we made the deal.

I was really enjoying this horse. Like I said, he traveled and handled exceptionally well. It was common for us to get our ropes out and rope brush as we rode down the trail or road. As soon as I started to loosen the strap that held my rope to my saddle, he freaked out and we nearly had a runaway! He'd been roped off alright and it wasn't pretty. I decided that he was going to be my branding horse for that spring. He couldn't run very far in the branding corral and after a hundred or so calves, he started to behave and made life easier on both of us. After that, he settled down and did pretty well the rest of the season.

We were gathering the Dragon City area when we had what I think could've been another angelic helper. Dragon City is an old ghost town where gilsonite ore was mined long ago. That area still has some old mine shafts that were either caved in or that were never covered in the first place. Well, Duke and I were in a high speed pursuit of an errant cow through the tall greasewood when suddenly a big black hole opened up in the ground in front of us. I remember thinking that if I tried to stop him, we were going in the hole, but if I spurred him, maybe he would be able to jump all the way across. He jumped and landed on the other side with his front end. After some serious scrambling, he made it all the way out. That one scared me!

I decided to ride him up Cottonwood a few miles from our place to see if I could catch a wild horse out of the bunch that was up there. I found them in a big open place that was surrounded by thick pinion pines and cedars. I quietly started riding toward the horses and they let me get about 125 yards away before they got nervous enough to turn and run. When they started to turn, I hooked the spurs to him and we took off. We were catching up to them in a hurry when they bailed off the hill into the trees. They were on a pretty good trail, but it was steep and so dry and dusty that I couldn't see anything but dust so I pulled him up to a stop. When the dust cleared, I saw that we were at the edge of a ledge and had we gone any further, I might not be writing this today.

Another time I tried chasing horses on him, I went with Bob and Gary Broome. We rode for quite a while until we spotted a bunch down below us on a steep open hillside. Gary and I took off after them and got in right behind them pretty quick. Gary roped a young stud and I was eating them up. The land leveled out some and we were going through some scattered trees. Duke decided to pass the horses rather than come up behind them to give me a chance at roping one. He'd been through this before evidently, and knew what was going on. I was pulling his head around to get him to turn closer and he just kept out of range going on past them! I marked up his right shoulder pretty well with my spur, but he wasn't moving over. I was so mad! There were still some in front of me and we hit a trail behind them. Again, it was pretty dusty and the next thing I knew, I caught a tree limb across my chest and was swept out of my saddle. All I could think of was getting run over by some of the horses we'd just outrun so I rolled up under a tree until the dust settled. They never came by so, fearing the worst, I thought I'd see if I could find my horse. He stopped not far down the trail and was waiting for me. My shirt was half ripped off and I was in a pretty foul mood. At least I still had my saddle and horse! I don't think I ever tried chasing horses on him again.

The next spring was just like the one before, he had to be trained to the rope all over again. My brother's father-in-law talked me into trading him for a really pretty 18 month old half wild filly and some tack. I used to wrangle horses on Duke bareback so when R W asked me to ride the horse bareback, I just bailed on and showed what he could do. When asked to lope, he complied, but wouldn't slow down when asked to stop until he got up to the fence. Then he stopped pretty quick and I sailed clear over the arena fence and landed on my back still gripping the reins and his nose smashed into the fence! That was the last time I got on him and I really didn't miss him much either!

The filly was small and like I said, she hadn't been handled much. I had her in one of the XIT stalls in Dalhart, Texas, which is where my brother lived at the time. (*He lived in town, not the stalls!*) Anyway, when I would clean her stall, I would lead her over to the arena. I was just getting her broke to lead and she was doing pretty well, but this time just before we got to the arena gate, she took off. I had a good hold on the lead rope and somehow stayed on my feet as she took me on some pretty good circles. It was a lot like water skiing except it was dirt and gravel. After a couple rounds, she stopped and faced me. She never pulled back again. I named her Angel.

Wolf Den Bull

We weaned the calves at the Jack Brewer place on Bitter Creek. Just before Christmas, we would trail them from there to the Park which generally took three days. I remember riding into the Park pasture on Christmas Eve long after dark and it was about 25 below zero. My right ear was frostbitten and swelled up pretty good. After getting everything situated, I went home to my folks place for a few days. My mom donated one of her nylon stockings to put on my head under my cowboy hat to keep my ear warm. It worked pretty well! I wore it until my ear healed up.

My next home was the Wolf Den cow camp. I was there alone most of the time and liked it that way. I was a long way from anybody with just my dog and horses. There were a couple wood cutting camps a few miles away but we generally didn't bother each other any. I was to check on the cows and just make sure things went well with them. The other job I had was to ride the four-year-old horses and kind of finish them off while turning them into usable stock horses during the course of the winter.

I had a big, stout buckskin gelding (*we didn't ride mares*) to ride named Judy. Yup, his name was Judy. He was named after his former owner. Anyway, he was big, gentle, tough and could really travel. One time Gary Smith and I were riding along and there was a couple feet of snow or more on the ground. I was on Judy and had to drop my rein on his neck to button my coat. About that time Judy decided to shake his head and my roping rein dropped on over his head. He just kept walking as I don't think he knew what had happened and wouldn't have cared anyway. Like I said earlier, he was a big horse and I'm not very big. When I reached up to grab my reins, I must have spurred him in the flanks because he took to bucking. And, according to Gary, he bucked hard! Well, I did a thorough job of sacking him out with my body before I performed a very ungraceful dismount into the snow. I still say that he didn't give me a fair chance! Oh well.

We noticed a young wild bull hanging around the cows and were hoping to gather him up some day. Well, one day I was riding Judy alone and just happened to see him with a small bunch of cows only about a mile from the camp. Thinking that this was the opportunity I was looking for, I started them toward the camp. At this time there was a lot of snow on the ground and everything pretty much followed trails to go anywhere. There was a good trail to camp so I thought this was going to work out just fine. After awhile some of the cows left on another trail but he with the others stayed on the right trail. A little further, the rest of the cows left him. He turned and looked at me like, "What are you going to do now?"

Well, I hollered and waved my arms at him and he went on a little further and stopped again and faced me. I hollered and waved my hands again. He wasn't impressed. I took down my rope and swung it around and howled some more. He went on a little further and stopped again, shaking his head and his six inch horns at me while blowing snot all over the snow, obviously showing his contempt and total disrespect for me or my great ideas. Generally, Hereford cattle aren't so aggressive that you have to worry about them hurting you while on horseback so I thought I'd call his bluff and charge him. It turned out not to be the greatest idea of the week or even the month, as he lowered his head and met us halfway.

We ended up in a pile all cuddled up together there in the snow. Now generally I'm not an overly quick thinker but thankfully, this was an exception. Judy got up and terminated the arrangement by rapidly going back to camp leaving the bull and me to work out our grievances together. I immediately realized that he was considerably bigger and meaner than I was. He was also faster and more mobile than I was in the deep snow. I was wearing floppy batwing chaps which aren't conducive for rapid travel whether you're in snow or on dry ground. I wasn't packing my pistol either. My dog, Red, was with me though, and he created enough of a diversion by chewing on the bull's back legs to keep him occupied long enough for me to get to a tree. There weren't any big enough to climb so I headed for the bushiest one I could find. The bull chased me round and round that tree until I was able to move to another tree. I had to try to keep a tree between the bull and me most of the way back to camp. He really wanted to hurt my feelings! After following me most of the way to camp, he finally got tired of the game and went on past so I was able to make it back to camp to find my faithless horse waiting by the fence.

That evening as I went back over the days happenings, it occurred to me that I had probably witnessed divine intervention on my behalf. After Judy left, I had no way to defend myself except to try to outrun the beast in two feet of snow while wearing floppy chaps and no gun. Thankfully Red, my dog, was there. I had been literally lying on top of the bull in the snow. I got the impression that the Lord had held him down just long enough for me to get away and there happened to be a fairly large, bushy tree to hide behind close by.

I was reminded of my patriarchal blessing I'd received nine years previous to this time. There were some promises in there that if I kept putting important things off, I'd miss out on. From that time forward, I started to change for the better. It's not that I was that bad, just that I could do a lot better if I changed some things in my life. That is when I decided to ask God if what I'd been told all my life was true. I knew it was, I just wanted a confirmation. I started to prepare to serve a mission and it has been a blessing ever since.

Barry's Bull

This isn't a horse story, but it's kind of related since cowboys need a bull to make calves so we can have things to do while we're horseback. My brother, Barry, had a big black, mean bull. I always kept a watch out while in the same pen or corral with him because I never knew if he would try to get me or not. One day Barry's wife, Temi, and I needed to move him from one pen to another and we were on foot which was less than ideal. I never knew him to charge a horse, but people on the ground seemed to be pretty tempting to him at times.

Anyway, Temi opened the gate to let him in the pen where I was. It was my job to guide him through a gate that I was standing next to. I had a little stick for intimidation and defense. Temi at least could hide behind her gate as she opened it. I was a wide open target. When she opened the gate, he came out, saw me and snorted his delight at finally getting a good shot at me and came at me with all the speed and determination he had. He wasn't intimidated by my little stick in the least. I heard Temi holler,"RUN!"

I don't know why she did that, because he was already running fast enough! She didn't need to encourage him! He was doing just fine on his own! I was stuck to the ground and couldn't move. Kind of like one of those dog soldiers I read about when they knew they were gonna die, but they drove their stake in the ground with the rope tied to it and the other end tied to their ankle facing overwhelming odds as the enemy came at them.

Here he came, the snot and foam flying from his nostrils and mouth, in a straight line for me. I tried to yell at him to at least get him to reconsider the evil designs he obviously had in executing his plan, and me in the process, but all that came out was a quiet little squeak. I showed him my stick hoping against hope that he would realize that if he killed me that God would punish him severely!

He increased his speed. The black demon-possessed beast lowered his head for the kill and then just before the impact, he veered off and barely missed me, but left stripes of snot and drool on my clothes! I think my angel had a bigger stick!

Heart Operation

Since I can't remember all the details, I'll have to try to go by what I think I can remember what I've been told about this thing. When I was just a two month old baby, our family was up on the mountain one day in July and my sister, Wanda, was watching over me while Mom set up the tent. I was in the truck with five year old Wanda close by. Dad had headed for the lake to go fishing. I was crying and Wanda couldn't get me to stop so she brought me to Mom. Mom got a little cross at her for packing me around until she realized that something was wrong when she saw that I was the wrong shade of blue. She gathered me up and headed down the trail to find Dad when she met a man and his wife coming up from the lake. The man took off back to the lake to get Dad while Mom and the lady went back to the truck and started taking down the camp. It was all loaded when Dad got there. By the time we got off the mountain, I was doing better, but Mom called the doctor anyway. He told her not to worry and to come see him in the morning. The next day, we found out that I had asthma and a heart murmur.

It was discovered that it was more than just a murmur. There were several things wrong with it that would require a two part surgery. The first was scheduled for early May at Primary Children's Hospital in Salt Lake City. I had an asthma attack and they waited for ten days hoping that they could get it under control. Finally, the doctor, who was a general authority in the Church over the young men, told Mom that they couldn't wait any longer. My heart that was supposed to be about the size of a turkey's heart, was about as big as Mom's fist and could burst any time. So, on my second birthday, they operated on me. I don't remember anything about that one. I have a scar around my left shoulder blade to remind me of it.

Mom told me that she got a reprimand from the Spirit while praying for me to get better. The impression she got was something like, "Who are you to order God?" She immediately asked for forgiveness. She said that she wasn't sure whether she'd see me alive again or not as they wheeled me through the doors to the operating room, but she wasn't worried. She felt things would be okay either way.

I do remember some of the second one. I was four years old and had been watching the television for a while and was familiar with some of the stuff in and around Salt Lake like Dee's Drive-in and others. So, when we drove through the city and I saw one, I was pretty excited! Kids! It was the mid '60's and the big hippie movement was in full swing. We were on our way to the hospital when I spotted a guy standing on the sidewalk with long hair. This was before all cars had air conditioning so the windows were down and I remember hollering to Mom over the noise of the car and wind asking if he was a hippie! She was so embarrassed! She shushed me and told me to be quiet!

I'd gotten a priesthood blessing from Elmer Bair, our stake patriarch, and was told that I would live to hold the priesthood and be able to take care of my elderly parents. Mom will turn 90 this year and I'm still waiting for her to be elderly! She has slowed down quite a bit though.

I had stitches in my forehead from an accident at home and I can recall lying in my hospital bed minding my own business when in came a black guy with a tray full of instruments. I'd never seen anyone but white people except on TV so it was kind of scary in real life! I tried to disappear into my sheets, but he still found me and took the stitches out without any more trauma. Having a TV in my own room was quite a deal for me. They'd bring my breakfast in the morning and gave up trying to retrieve the dirty dishes until they brought my lunch in to me because I'd eat a bite, watch some TV, eat a bite, watch TV...

Mom was there as much as she could be, but night time was mighty lonely for a four year old boy a long way from home and people he knew. I remember one night as I lay in my bed, I was crying and a mean, old, chunky night nurse came into my room and said, in a loud, obnoxious voice, "SHUT UP! YOU'RE WAKING ALL MY PEOPLE!"

I shut up. At least on the outside, and she strutted off thinking that she'd done the world a great service by bullying a little boy.

I remember waking up during the surgery. They had opened up my chest and I remember hearing the sounds of the room and could feel things moving in my chest and wondered if I should open my eyes. Someone must've been paying attention because that's all I remember! Mom tells me that she was told that I was only the fifth person to live through this operation. Surgeons all over America and Europe were researching this situation and method. I remember the surgeon's name was Dr. Veasy. I don't know if that's the correct spelling, but that's what it sounds like.

They must have done a good job because it never gave me any more trouble after that. I remember we had Field Day toward the last of the school year in grade school. That was the only part of school that I liked at the time. We ran races and just generally had fun outside. Cally Steele and I were the undefeated three legged race champions. We never lost a race together. One year, I think it was my fourth grade year, the family doctor found out about my heart operation and forbid me to take part in field day. It was tough watching the other kids out doing what I wanted to do and couldn't. I went on to participate in all activities that any other healthy kid did after that without any trouble.

Our family seemed to be fairly social back then. Whenever we would go to someone's home, inevitably Dad would call me over and have me lift up my shirt to show off my battle scars. Those scars represented a lot of things to my parents. We still have copies of the bills.

Bear Roping

I'm not sure whether to include this one in the guardian angel category or to just plain good horse sense. I'm leaning toward the latter. This happens to be one of the few instances where I actually made the right decision before a wreck!

Wade and I were working for the Cripple Cowboy and I can't recall whether it was spring or fall, but the grass was yellow, it was warm and we were staying at the Jack Brewer cow camp on Bitter Creek. We were down the canyon on the Frank Brewer place . There were remnants of an irrigation ditch in front of us about 75 yards away and I saw a brown head sticking up above the grass about the size of a big coyote. I pulled up my horse and Wade came up next to us when I pointed it out. It must've heard us because the coyote stood on its hind legs to get a look at us. It wasn't a coyote at all, it was a young bear that was about three feet tall while standing on its back legs. After a little while it dropped down to all fours and ambled off into a thick stand of brush.

"Pretty neat!, I said after it disappeared.

"I want a closer look", Wade said.

"You just got a closer look," I said.

"No, I want to get close!"

Well, I'm not too smart but I am fairly frugal and the rope I was packing was nearly new and I had no plans on giving it up to a bear and said so to Wade.

He was pretty determined to rope this little bear and it would look pretty cool on a resume if the little feller didn't have a mom anywhere close by. I was wondering how he was planning on getting his rope off if he did manage to catch it. I told him that I would chase it to him, but after that, he was on his own. He agreed and got set for the chase.

I've been told that a bear can outrun a quarterhorse for a ways, but Wade was riding Parrot and Parrot could really move for a short distance, so this could get interesting! Wade had his rope down and his loop built when I hollered and my horse and I crashed into the brush where we'd watched the bear go into earlier. It came out right next to Wade just like a calf coming out of the chute in an arena. There was about a hundred yards to the trees and safety for the bear. Wade and Parrot were catching up to it pretty quick when I think Parrot had more sense than his rider and stayed just out of roping range the rest of the way! Wade and I were talking about this a few years later when he made the comment that it wasn't the smartest thing he's ever done. It seems the word "crazy" was used. I agreed!

The Swimming Hole

This one doesn't have anything to do with horses, but it still, I think, has something to do with divine intervention.

One day several of my friends and I decided to go swimming in the river on a part of the ranch. I knew of a place that looked to be deep enough to actually swim in so that's where we went. It had some current in it that had a slow circular pattern that didn't allow it to fill up with sediment. It also had a spot that literally dropped straight off and was fairly deep. In fact, Nelson dove straight down just a couple feet away from the bank and came up with a stripe of mud on the bridge of his nose! He thought we were all messing with him until he actually wiped his nose off and saw the mud! We all got a pretty good laugh out of that one!

It's not uncommon to see small whirlpools where the slow water comes up against the faster water. In summertime when the water is lower, it's not usually a concern and it was something I never even thought of. We were all just playing around in the water not really paying attention to danger signs from anyone. Anyway, I swam out to that edge and realized that I wasn't going anywhere. I swam harder and still couldn't get any closer to the bank. I kept at this until I was about ready to give up.

No one noticed my struggles and I was so out of breath by the time I realized the trouble I was in that I couldn't call out. I was in a lot of trouble and there wasn't anyone to help. I remember giving one final effort and broke free of the current and making it back to the bank where I dragged myself out and just sat there for a long time. I had nothing left. I got the impression then, and still do that I was helped out by someone I couldn't see. I don't swim in the river any more.

The Dream

I don't think this story has anything to do with divine intervention, but it's interesting to me anyway. I was a sophomore in high school and my wrestling season was over. I'd been on junior varsity all year and had lost about as many matches as I'd won. I wasn't much to fear. After the last practice before the district tournament, I turned in all my gear and went home. The next day was Friday and it was the first day of the two day tournament.

Those going to the event got out of school early so they could travel, get weighed and settled in. I wasn't worried because I wasn't going. I had dinner and then went to bed.

My bedroom was converted from half a garage about twenty yards away from the house. The girls slept in the house. That night I dreamt that Coach Klements called and wanted to know if I was interested in taking Kevin's place in the tournament. He caught a case of the mumps and was unable to go. His weight class was about ten pounds heavier than mine. I didn't think anything of it until I came in for breakfast the next morning.

Like every morning, Mom would holler at me from the house that it was time to get up and I'd holler back that I was coming. As I came into the house, she said that Coach Klements had called and wanted me to call him back. Well, that was interesting! I called him up and he said that Kevin was sick and couldn't make it to the tournament, would I be interested in taking his place? Wow! Exactly as it had happened in my dream! I told him I'd go and told my mom what had just happened.

As luck would have it, there were nine wrestlers in the weight class and I had to wrestle just to be in the regular tournament. My dad actually came to watch me. We were in Glenwood Springs two hours from home! I think his buddy Walt talked him into going. But he came! I don't think he'd ever gone to watch me wrestle before. Now he came to watch me be fed to the lions. I was 14 pounds lighter than anyone in my class, and when you only weigh 105 pounds, that's quite a percentage. I tried to weigh in fully dressed with my coat and boots but they wouldn't let me!

My first match was with a kid from Aspen. As I was getting ready to step out onto the mat, I said to Coach, "I can beat this guy".

"Sure you can!", came the obligatory response.

Well, I beat him 10-1 with my dad watching! The next match was when the lion showed up. He was the number one seed for good reason. I made it to the second period before he pinned me, but he had to work for it.

Dad went home that night but was listening on the radio the next day for my next match. It was against a kid from Craig and the radio station broadcasting was from Craig too. This time I made it to the third period before getting pinned, but the announcers—according to Dad—really praised me for never quitting.

Now, did my dad expect me to win the tournament? No. He came because I was wrestling there obviously and I'm sure Walt talked him into going, but he was proud of me for trying my best. That makes the difference to me.

I think God has a similar attitude toward us. He knows us better than we know us. He knows we will fail at times, but He's always there to cheer us on and encourage us to do our best. Just like my dad, He wants us to do our best, get up when we fall and keep trying.

Post Mission Life

The Coal Mine

After nearly starving to death driving a truck in the oil field, I was offered a job at the local underground coal mine. It paid a lot more, plus it had great benefits, something my previous employer had promised for a couple years instead of a raise but never delivered on either of them. I never considered working there until I saw that staying where I was wasn't ever going to pay the bills and allow any savings to build up. I stayed there eight long, dark years until we were financially stable enough to live on a reduced income. I grew to hate Sundays because I knew I'd have to be back in that dark hole that night or the next day. I had bills to pay and a family to take care of. Their needs took precedence over my wants. I never resented them for it, but I was sure envious of their freedom.

My first couple years were working the graveyard shift which was 11pm to 7am. One winter morning while driving home after work, I fell asleep. I was driving my pickup truck and had just dozed off when I felt something was wrong. I was asleep! That's what was wrong! I woke up just as I was headed off the left side of the road. Thankfully, no one was coming. That spot has about a 10-15 foot drop off before it levels out. There were a few inches of snow on the ground and I realized in a split second that I had two options. The first one was if I tried to correct and swerve back onto the road, the truck would roll. The second was to turn off the road quickly, go down the steep embankment and I'd be fine. I was going fast enough that when I cranked the wheel as hard as I could I only left one tire track on the passenger side in the snow until I hit the bottom. The driver's side tires never touched the ground until we got to the bottom. The truck and I were completely unscathed. I put the truck in four wheel drive, drove to a less steep spot and got back on the road and went home! A few days later, as I was going to town I noticed a guy stopped there looking at the one track going down the hill. I kept going!

I worked all over the coal mine as time went by and had the opportunity to run everything except the continuous miner. That was fine with me as I preferred to be what is called "outby"; that's when you are not in the development sections where the actual coal is being cut out and shipped out on a series of conveyor belts. The development sections are "inby", pronounced out-by and in-by. I was in the section and we were moving the continuous miner to another mining face or entry. It takes several people to do this. One with a remote control to operate the miner, and a couple or more to watch out for the miner cable which is just a power cord that runs from the power center to the miner. The cable is about 2½"-3" thick and heavy. When backing out of the mining face, the cable is looped on the tail of the miner. The tail is a steel rail with a conveyor chain in it that can move up and down as well as from side to side. It dumps the coal that the miner digs out of the coal vein into the buggy that then takes it to the stamler which happens to be the end of the conveyor belt in the section.

We had a new-to-us operator and I was still used to the former operator that always kept aware of where everyone was. This guy didn't and I should have watched him more than trusting him like I had the other guy. As the miner swung around on its' tracks, I was hanging another loop of cable on the tail. It swung around and pinned me against the wall or rib as they're called.

I flashed my light around trying to catch anyone's eye before it crushed me. Thankfully, he saw me and shut things down. I didn't even get scratched. If that machine would have wiggled just a little, I could have been severely injured or killed. While I worked there those years, two good men lost their lives. One left a young family of, I think, six or eight children. The other was getting ready to retire. I knew both of them. Underground coal mining is a dangerous occupation with a lot of injuries. Some obviously serious. I never want to do that again. Thankfully, I'm old enough that they won't let me anyway!

Horse and Cowboy Stories

The next stories aren't about being protected as far as I know, but are just things that I think are interesting and kind of fun.

Broken Foot

I was riding what's called a green broke mare which only means that she hadn't been ridden much and was leading another mare with other horses following us up the river to some pasture that hadn't been used much. It was the second of December and there were a couple inches of wet snow on the ground. I wanted to utilize this pasture as long as I could so I wouldn't have to feed as much hay through the winter. As we were starting down a small slope, I had the lead rope dallied around my saddle horn when the mare I was leading pulled back and jerked the mare I was riding off her feet. She fell on my right foot before I could get free and then they all took off.

When I stood up I knew, something was wrong. My foot was hurting and I was close to a mile away from the house. The horses had stopped about 150 yards away so I hobbled over and caught my saddle horse and rode home. While walking to the horses I could feel what I thought were bones rubbing against each other. After I got home, I was able to pull my boot off and I thought I could feel the end of a bone sticking up out of place on the right side of the instep of my foot. I thought to myself, "If it's broke now, it'll still be broke tomorrow". So I went to bed.

Mom hauled me to the doctor the next day and sure enough, it was broke. I got to wear a plaster cast for a while. On Christmas Eve, I cut it off as a present to myself and it must have healed up pretty well because it's never given me any trouble since then.

The Relay Race

Every year around Memorial Day, Rangely would have the Rangely Days Rodeo. It was the only one of the year and we looked forward to it. There were the usual events, but since there was a race track there, we looked forward to the saddle horse races.

It was maybe a couple weeks before the rodeo and Wade and I were talking about it when I mentioned that it was too bad that no one got any relay teams together. "Well Hank's been training one for two weeks now," Wade said. I didn't know of anyone else that was putting one together so I told Wade that I'd ask around and if nobody else had one, that I'd put one together just for the show. At the time, I had no idea how prophetic those words would be.

I couldn't find anyone who had planned to get a team together, so a couple days before the rodeo, I gathered up my fat saddle horse and pulled a mostly broke brood mare out of the pasture. I still needed a horse so I asked Bob Broome if he'd be willing to let me borrow his horse. He was willing and even offered to help, which was great because you need people to hold and catch the horses during the course of the race. I still needed another helper and Tim decided to be the victim.

The general plan for the relay race consisted of three legs with the first two running a quarter mile and the last running one lap around the track which ended up being a half mile and ending in front of the grand stands. There's some strategy involved in placing your horses. You want a quick start with the slower horse in the middle and the long running horse last to make up ground if the other two get outrun.

Well, I was going to start on Angel. She's the horse I traded for in Texas that was doing really well. I'd never raced her and I don't know if I ever asked her to run full out before, but I felt like she should have some speed. I asked Hank if it was okay if we started from a walk as I didn't know if she'd buck by taking off from a standing start. He agreed and when he hollered "GO" away we went.

Well, the first thing she did was to bog her head and try to buck. The funny thing was, while she was doing this, she was still outrunning Hank! I got her head up and she really took off! She could fly! When we got to the change out on the backstretch behind the announcers stand, we were a good fifty yards in front. I got her to stop without smashing Tim up too much and swung onto Skeets, my trusty broke saddle horse. But when I poked him with my spurs, he bucked me off in front of everybody!

He'd never offered to buck before or since, but he did then. Meanwhile, Hank caught up and swung onto his horse and was well on his way before I ran down and caught Skeets and got headed in the right direction. He still thought it would be fun to unload me in this time of expediency but I kept his head up and like Angel, settled down to run with a purpose.

By this time, Hank had about 150 yards on me and as I came up for the last change, I watched as he went to swing onto his last horse. He must've been full of adrenalin because when he went to jump on, he jumped clear over and landed on the other side of his horse! I thought to myself, "I'll catch him!" By the time he got on his way, he wasn't too far in front. I bailed off

Skeets and went to get on Bobs big, tall horse. I was tired! Bob picked me up and in the saddle I went, and away we went. That horse could really run and when I asked him for speed, he didn't hold anything back! We caught and passed Hank before he made it out of the first turn and then just coasted the rest of the way.

It turned out to be a show, alright. Not exactly what I had planned, though! Horse races are always fun!

The Lost Lariats

The first summer after our son got home from his mission, we went camping up in the mountains. We always brought the horses to ride. One day we decided to go to a small lake called Anderson reservoir. There are two ways to get there from our camp. The easy way is to drive up the road to the trailhead and go the mile or so up the mountain to the lake. The other way is just that…a way. The first mile or so from our camp spot is pretty good, as there's a decent trail to follow. Then the trail disappears and you have to find your own way and I've never gone the same way twice.

This happened to us again and as we were thrashing around in the brush and trees, Landon realized his lariat was gone. This happened right after my horse decided to cut under a dead tree that was just low enough for him to fit under with absolutely no consideration for me or my welfare. It was like a huge comb with the dead branches scraping me from one end to the other resulting in a very unhappy and grumpy rider! When Landon mentioned that he'd lost his rope, I looked down and saw that mine was gone too. With all the brush we'd gone through, I knew there was no way we were ever going to see them again. We backtracked the best we could with no success when Landon suggested we pray. I was still in a pretty foul mood and told him to go ahead.

After the prayer, we got up, walked a few paces and there were our ropes all coiled up nice leaning up against a log like someone put them there. We looked around, knowing that we were alone, but looking just the same and picked them up. We never heard anyone else, nor did we ever see anyone else, and no one could have gotten that close to us without one of us noticing them.

Now, I've dropped my rope before and it NEVER stays coiled up. It always strings out a ways. Then to have both of them all coiled up neatly and sitting side by side against a tree trunk laying on the ground right next to the trail we'd just walked by? Pretty neat!

Buster

I'd been breaking colts for a while and my reputation was being circulated around that I kinda knew what I was doing. As a result, people would call me up wanting me to get their horse started. I could usually tell if the horse had had a bad experience pretty quickly. Buster was one of these. The owner said that he just didn't have the time to work with this horse and asked me to get him going. Buster was a pig-eyed buckskin three year old gelding. Generally, a pig-eyed horse has an attitude to start with and can be a little tougher to deal with. At least that's been my experience with all those I've dealt with. It was spring time and a little windy. Sometimes that can mess with their attitude and make them a little more jumpy than they would be normally. I worked with him for three days in the corral getting on and off, asking him to move out, turning and stopping etc. and he was doing really well even with the wind, so I decided to take him outside.

It didn't take long with all that room in front of him to decide to do something stupid. I could feel his back start to bow up and watched as his ears started to twitch back and forth and as he started to look around I knew he was about to buck. He didn't buck really hard but probably enough to scare his owners into getting someone else to do what they really didn't want to do in the first place.

When he couldn't buck me off, he ran away, which is sometimes worse. He ran all the way around our 100 acre field, under tree branches, across ditches and all. When we got back to the corral, I knew I had to do something else. My dad had plowed a field up and I decided that it would work perfectly for what I wanted to do.

I took him into that rough ground and got on and off him, walked him around in circles and generally made sure he had to watch his step. He stumbled around a lot and couldn't do anything but try to stay upright. Each day I would take him a little further in the field and sometimes out of the field. When I felt he was ready for it, I took him on about a 15 mile ride. After climbing a pretty long hill, we got to an open area that didn't have any real obstacles so I decided to try to get him to lope a ways. Well, that ended up being a lot of work because he knew he wasn't supposed to run away! It took close to half a mile to get into a lope and he was doing pretty well when my left stirrup fell off. I got him shut down , turned around and went back and picked it up. I was able to slide off his left side, reattach my stirrup and away we went. After a month I took him back and I don't think he was ever ridden again.

Cow Patty

We had a county extension agent named Patricia. Of course, kids being kids renamed her Cow Patty. Not with her knowledge or consent, I'm sure. She leased a three year old Arabian mare with part of the lease agreement being that the mare be trained to ride. Some people don't care for the term "broke", but it's all the same to me.

The mare was halter broke (*trained!*), but that was all. She was a little wild and I figured I had my work cut out for me with this one. Wade made the comment that the reason most people have a hard time with Arabians is that the horses are smarter than the people that are trying to train them. If she was any example of this, I'll have to agree. She was smart.

I thought I'd have to tie up a back foot to saddle her, but she kicked out of it so I tried without the rope and she did just fine. Because she was so smart, she was fun to work with. In two weeks she was neck reining really well and by the time Cow Patty came to ride her two weeks after that, she had "power steering".

Patty asked if she could use spurs to ride her and I told her that the mare didn't need them, that she had power steering. Well, Cow Patty put them on anyway. We'd ridden half a mile or so when I heard a commotion behind me. I turned around and saw Cow Patty hanging halfway off the horse with both hands in a death grip around the saddle horn and eyes the size of silver dollars with her mouth wide open! After crawling back up into the saddle, she commented that she really DID have power steering! Yup, told ya so!

Ranger

Ranger came to us as a gentle, unbroken eight year-old gelding. He was the last living progeny of my stud Leggy. He is out of a racing mare that was more thoroughbred than quarterhorse, throw in more of that along with 25% Arabian and there he is. He really likes to travel and can cover a lot of country in a hurry if you ask him to.

When we got him the previous owners' said that they couldn't do anything with him. I saddled him up with no trouble but after getting on him, I couldn't get him to move out. Finally, I got my son on him and started leading him around. He got the idea and really moved on from there. I teach my horses to move away from pressure so it makes sense to them when I'm teaching them to neck rein. Lots of times, I can drop the reins and get to where I want to go by just using leg pressure. This came in really handy once.

I was riding the river bottoms checking cows and conditions when I found a bull elk that had died the fall or winter before. He had a really nice six point rack of antlers on him. I didn't have a saw to cut them off with me so I had to come back another time. I was riding Ranger when I made it back and cut the horns off then had to figure out how to hold onto them and keep him under control as he liked to get back as quickly as I'd let him. Well, I hung them on a limb, got on Ranger and grabbed the horns, set them on my shoulders with a hand on each beam and laid the reins on Ranger's neck. I wasn't too worried about going up over the mountain, but I was concerned that as soon as we started down the mountain toward the house he would want to hurry and I wouldn't have any control over anything.

He never tried anything and responded exactly to each of my leg requests. We zig- zagged down the mountain better than when I held the reins! He knew. He's one of the best horses I've ever had, and I've been blessed with some really good ones.

Bailey

We each had three horses in our string to ride at the Cripple Cowboy and Bailey was one in my string. He was a lean, buckskin colored horse of average size with a little bit of a Roman nose. He was an alright kind of horse and did enough to get the job done.

It was spring time and we were getting ready for the spring roundup and branding. All of us cowboys would stay at the Jack Brewer place on Bitter Creek while we gathered the cows and branded their calves before we turned them up the creek to the mountain for the summer.

One of us always went up a week or so earlier and killed an elk to eat while we stayed there. We didn't consider it poaching, just subsistence hunting. I was elected to do the job and went up Augusi Canyon and did just that. The elk I killed was an old cow that happened to give me the best shot. She died up the hill in a sandstone rock pile. I thought I'd just get Bailey to haul the quarters down to the road where I could load them into my truck. Gary Broome told me that Bailey had packed elk before so I had no worries.

He didn't seem too impressed that he was elected to help out with this particular job. I tied one hind quarter to the saddle horn on his right side with no trouble and had to use a smaller rope to tie the other quarter on the other side. As I started to lead him down the hill to the truck, I noticed he had a look in his eyes that didn't look good so I stepped to the side and tugged on the reins a little to get him to untrack. And boy did he ever untrack! He bucked so hard that the quarters would fly up in the air and come down with a WHUMP nearly knocking the air out of him. He would reach out while bucking and bawling and take a bite of the elk leg and shake it until the mouthful came out, then do it again. Oh he was mad! Finally one of the ropes broke and he stopped bucking but stood there shaking. I took the quarter off and tied my lariat to it and stepped into the saddle and dallied my rope around the saddle horn. When I asked him to move, he bogged his head again and tried to buck. He found out that it's a lot harder to buck with a drag holding him down! We got the quarters down to the road without any further incident.

Cuttin' Tommy aka Kalijah

Tommy was going to be four years old come spring and he was already a big stout horse. He was pretty, too. Big bay with a splash of white on his face and maybe even on a foot or two, I don't remember for sure. And like all the ranch horses, he had a white 65 freeze branded on his left shoulder. I was going to the Wolf Den camp for the winter and Tommy was one of the horses I had to ride. Since I was by myself most of the time, Jon told me to never ride this horse alone. Gary Smith came out for a while and we took a pretty good ride while I was on Tommy.

I had to peddle that lazy horse the whole way and it would have been easier on me to walk all that way rather than ride him! Spring time came and we needed to gather the cows out of the Park, the winter headquarters, and head them down the canyon to Evacuation Creek where they would work their way to the mountain after we branded the calves. We were going to be there for a few days so I thought it would be a good experience for Tommy to have a steady job since the opportunity was there.

Gary had his two little girls staying there and he would take them through the pasture in his truck to check the heifers while they were calving. One day, I decided to check them on Tommy. I got on him and he decided he wasn't going to be lazy that day and we checked them on the run without my consent! I decided that if he had that much energy, we could go and check on some other cows so I rode over to the trailer we stayed in to let Gary know what I was up to. Tommy was still being a mess and I was getting tired of it so I hooked him with my spurs in his front end and he took to bucking! He bucked really nice and even so I took my hat off and fanned him while he was bucking. That's the only time I ever tried that... but I had an audience!

The day came to head the cows and their calves down the canyon. Jon, Gary, and I saddled up and started the gather. I was on Tommy and was following a small calf that wasn't doing too well so I thought I'd get off and just walk behind him to keep Tommy from stepping on him. As I swung my leg over the saddle to get off, Tommy jumped out from under me and took off, leaving me sprawled out in the sagebrush.

Gary caught him and brought him back. I don't know where the calf went so I got back on and joined the herd. A cow cut back and I turned Tommy to bring her back and he took to bucking. After hopping around a while, he gave up and started following the cows. He tried a couple more times as we went down the canyon, but couldn't get me off.

We got about halfway down the canyon and decided to let the cows and calves take a rest break. But that's where the battle really came to a head. I didn't dare get off for fear that he'd try to kick me or some other nefarious action. He and I went at it all the time everyone else was resting. He would buck until he was out of breath, stop and get his wind back and have at me again. I was using a roping rein so when he dropped his head, he'd nearly pull me out of the saddle and I'd have to grab the cantle of my saddle to stay on. By the time we made it back to the Park, we were both pretty tired. I told Jon that I was tired of riding that...horse.

Jon ended up having me take him to the sale in Roosevelt, Utah, since, after that, no one else wanted to ride him either! There was a rodeo stock contractor named O'Driscol at the sale. I told him about Tommy but someone else outbid him. A couple months later, Jon was talking to a BLM guy and the man mentioned that he thought he'd seen one of Jons horses in the rodeo arena. After describing the horse, it was evident that it was Tommy. This was a week or so after the rodeo in Vernal and there were three guys that were going to try this horse out as a saddle bronc. The first guy lasted a jump and fell off. The next did about the same. The third had won the saddle bronc riding the week before and lasted three jumps before getting dumped. The BLM guy asked Jon what he did with the horse before this.

"My cowboys punched cows on him! " Jon said.

He walked away shaking his head!

Skeets

I went down to visit my brother Barry in Texas for a while. Those people down there are the tradingest bunch I've ever seen! I was riding a 14" saddle and a big ole boy was trying to trade me out of it. He couldn't even fit one leg in it, let alone sit in it! Tradin' is fun.

I was kind of in the market for a saddle horse. The outfit Barry worked for had a nice pretty sorrel horse for a pretty decent price. He'd come off the track and had a lot of speed as well as handling fairly well. There was another horse, a two year old untouched red dun colt that was a little straight shouldered and not very big that we looked at. He cost quite a bit less, so I bought him hoping we could get along. He was a registered quarter horse named Skeets Cody Leo. His pedigree showed a lot of cowhorse. He was really smart. I started him with a bosal and later switched to a snaffle bit. That was a challenge. He did not like anyone touching his mouth. We would wrestle around for half an hour with me trying to get that thing in his mouth. Finally, he realized that if he just opened his mouth, I wouldn't touch his mouth. Everything was that way. Once I showed him what I wanted him to do, he had it figured out. He never offered to buck—except during the relay race!

Like I said, he wasn't very big and I had him in with some of Jon Hills yearlings when he was about 30 months old when Ben Steele came to visit. Jon was showing his colts off and then said, "That THING there is Layne's."

I felt that was pretty uncalled for. He would later eat those words.

Skeets learned quickly and never forgot. He trusted me and I trusted him. He could run a lot faster than he looked. He had a great neck rein and would really watch a cow. One time when we were going along a fence line, there was a bull on the other side going the same way. I wasn't really paying that much attention to him so when he turned back and Skeets turned back, I nearly fell off! Skeets was watching him and wasn't going to let him get away!

One day Jon was riding Coon, his stud horse that had been in cow cutting training for a while. We were sorting cattle at Jacks place and I was riding Skeets. I thought Skeets outperformed that "pretty" horse hands down. Later, Jon asked if one of Fran's (his wife) boys could ride him when we trailed the calves to the Park because he handled so well. I guess he didn't think the ranch horses fit the bill.

One time a friend and I went out chasing wild horses. I roped a three year old albino stud and was bringing him back to the truck when I dropped my tie fast (chain link) off my rope into the brush. I asked my friend if he'd pick it up for me. He poked around a little and said he couldn't see it. I tied a couple half hitches around my saddle horn, got off, dropped my reins and walked back 25 yards and picked it up while Skeets stood there and held that horse. My friend was pouting because he got outrun and I caught a horse.

I could shoot from my saddle without any trouble or get off, drop the reins and shoot around him. He never left me. I loaded half an elk on him and tied his lead rope up and he followed me wherever I went. He packed deer and camp without any trouble. He was my first really good horse. I feel fortunate to have owned and ridden him.

Wild Horse Circus

It seems like whenever the Allreds and I get together, things never go as smoothly as they do for anyone else. This was one of those times. It was after Christmas around New Years and it was cold. I had a few days break and invited Wade to come with me chasing wild horses. Of course he said yes so we headed to the Park.

We'd just brought the calves in after a three day trail drive from the Jack Brewer place on Bitter Creek to the Park Christmas Eve. It was -25 degrees and my right ear was pretty frostbitten and swelled up when we got in way after dark. I'd spent a couple days with my folks at their place and was ready to get out of the house, even with a frostbitten ear. My mom donated a nylon stocking to help keep my ear warm and it helped a lot!

Anyway, I was riding a buckskin colored ranch horse named Injun that I was getting to like quite a bit. We spotted a small group of three horses down below us. We snuck down to 'em, got our ropes down and headed their way at a walk. When they saw us, they took off with us right on their heels. The mare and the stud quickly peeled off into the trees, but we were able to get between them and their two year old colt. He headed out toward a rocky rim with no way off. There was a big rock about the size of a big truck that the horse would have to go around on his way back. Wade stationed himself next to it with his rope hanging out so when the horse came by, Wade would just stick it out and the horse would get caught. Easy, right? He missed! Well, now it's my turn. I catch up to him and I'm wearing a new hat and I really have to rock my head back to see to throw my rope. I missed! Here comes Wade. I'm literally bumping this horse with my foot trying to guide him and at the same time hollering to Wade to hurry up since it's his turn! He throws a good loop but didn't pull the slack out and as his horse runs by, pulls the rope off! I didn't miss my next time. I think the horse was glad someone either caught him or left him alone! I took him to the same sale that Tommy went to and got $25 for him. He wasn't halter broke or anything and as I was leaving the sale barn pens, I saw a man and his young daughter trying to corner him to halter and take him home. I hope they got their moneys worth!

Bob Laying Down on the Job

Bob Broome was kind of my second dad when it came to horses. He and I went chasing wild horses several times together. He taught me a lot about horses and cattle on our rides together. We were in the Yanks and Fletcher area east of Rangely looking for horses. That's some rugged, rough country at a walk not to mention on a dead run on horseback. We'd chased some without catching up to any and Bob was on a trail a ways in front of me when I was able to chase some horses his way.

My horse was spent and it looked like they were going to run right past him. Bob was over six feet tall and always rode a tall horse so I could see his head sticking up over the cedar trees. I hollered at him to get ready and watched as he got his rope ready and hunkered down. A few seconds later, I heard a crash and some limbs breaking so I figured he probably caught one.

I don't know if I was prepared for what I saw when I got there. He roped the black 750 pound mare as she was going past him at top speed while his horse was facing the trail. When she hit the end of the rope, he was broadside and tied hard and fast which means the end of his rope was tied to the saddle horn. She jerked his horse over on his side and she was stretched out on the ground with the rope so tight it wasn't touching the ground between them. Bob was trapped under his horse and none of them could move. He still had his hat on along with that big smile while watching me come up the trail. Bob's horse's feet were sticking out in the air over the small ledge he was standing next to. The rope was still tied to the saddle horn and that kept Bob's horse from getting up and the mare still had little tweety birds flying around her head from the sudden stop! I was able to help get everybody upright and kind of back to normal. That horse hit the end of the rope so hard that Bob lost one of his spurs from the crash and we were never able to find it. The things we do for fun!

The Test Ride

One morning when I went out to do the chores, there was a big, pretty Appaloosa stud out by the corrals. I had no idea where he came from or who he belonged to, but Ginger, our mare, was in heat so I put them in the same pen together with my dad's permission. A few days later, Jack Brown came down to the Ranch and saw his horse in the pen and was glad to finally find him! We didn't even know he owned a horse.

Fast forward a couple years and the result of this union was a very beautifully colored bay Appy colt that had terrible conformation. But he was pretty colored! He was also pretty wild. I decided to break him so I started working with him. Like I said, he was kind of wild so I took my time and worked with him on the ground for a couple weeks. He never let me get my foot in the stirrup without taking off. I got impatient and decided I was getting on that horse whether he liked it or not. I worked him around and around until he was standing a little better, then I went to swing up on him and he jumped. I landed behind the saddle and was riding him pretty well while he bucked real pretty until we got to the fence. He turned, I didn't, and ended up cracking some ribs.

Dad was working with a guy who claimed he could break him so Dad sent him that way. He brought him back a couple weeks later unbroken. He said the horse bucked him off. Well, I thought we might have a rodeo stock prospect so I took him up to the rodeo grounds to try him out. Wade would be my helper. I thought I'd try to get on him in the arena and he stood there and let me on! I was surprised to say the least! When I asked him to go, he went! He hit a high lope which may have actually been his top speed! He would start to lean like he was going to turn right and when I started to lean into the turn, he'd duck back the other way so quickly that I found myself hanging onto the saddle horn way out in space! Then he'd try the other way with the same tactic. He never bucked, just turned really quick. This went on for quite a while until I decided he was never going to be a rodeo bronc. I didn't know what to do with him now.

I was working at the grocery store cutting meat at the time and I'd get to visit with people throughout the day. One day, Chris Cubbs came in. He was working for Jon Hill at the time so naturally the talk turned to horses. I told him about this horse and he sounded interested so we set up a time for him to come look at him. He showed up and looked him over and asked some more questions. I told him all the history I knew about the horse then he said that he wanted to ride him. You what? Yup, he wanted to saddle him up and take him for a ride. I went through the story again thinking I'd left something out. He wanted to ride that horse. Okay! This should be fun. You want to ride him outside the corral? In the brush?! Okay, I'll saddle my horse too.

Chris was a Vietnam vet and had a bad right knee. it was pretty stiff and wouldn't bend much. He got his saddle on without any trouble and the horse wouldn't let him on so I grabbed one of the horses ears and twisted and chomped down on it like I'd heard the old time cowboys did. When Chris swung up in the saddle, I was lifted clear off my feet when the horse reared up. I guess this horse didn't know that trick was supposed to work. They made a big swing out through the greasewood and tamarack with Skeets and I following close behind then they started on another circle going the same way so I stopped and waited for them to come back by. They didn't come. I went looking and found the rider-less horse and eventually a mud covered Chris.

They'd made it to the river when the horse did one of his patented quick turns and deposited Chris in the mud next to the river. He still wanted to ride this horse. Knowing that the age old ear trick wasn't going to work, I dallied him up so his nose (the horse's, not Chris) was literally in my lap. Chris swung up and the horse reared up and I was looking up.

Chris got settled in and was on the move with absolutely no control over his direction or his destiny because that horse was headed for a low hanging tree limb that was just about the right height to sweep Chris out of the saddle. I could see the evil intent so we hustled up to avoid what appeared to be a messy cleanup job about to happen. Just before reaching the tree, we knocked both of them out of dangers path.

I thought it would be safer to head up the Cottonwood road to avoid any traffic. Skeets, my saddle horse, was really smart and caught on quickly. He figured out that they were supposed to stay on the road. We loped along behind them and after a while when they'd start to veer off, he'd run up and push them over to the middle of the road then back off until they needed more guidance We went up a couple miles and got them turned around and made it back to the corrals without any further incident.

"I'll take him", he said.

"Really? After all that? Great ! I hope you'll both be very happy together!"

He took the horse to the Wolf Den to ride that winter and Fran, Jon's wife, told me that they came to check on him one day and saw him riding "Oddball" as he was named, in the round pen seemingly doing well. A few minutes later a tired and worn Chris came in and told them how glad he was to see them because he'd been trapped on that horse for over an hour! I guess he eventually ended up making a decent horse out of him after all.

Fasting and Fast Cows

I had a small bunch of cows, ten cows and calves with a young bull, to be specific. I enjoyed them most of the time and they gave my horses and me something to do. I liked watching the calves grow and the chance they gave me to get out and unwind while horseback after making a living in the oilfield every day. It seemed as though that they were getting a little harder to handle every year, even after I built new fences to keep them where I wanted them to stay. The problem was the river.

It's considered a navigable river here and so I'm not allowed to run a fence across. The cows just walked around the fence and up the river and went wherever they wanted to go. This caused problems with the neighbors. They aren't stock people and haven't the faintest idea about livestock or their habits. Nor do they want to. I decided that the best course of action would be to get rid of them to try to get along. Besides, our son Landon was grown and gone and I was having a harder time doing things that needed done alone.

A few friends and I saddled up and went after them one day. The river bottoms are thickly covered with Russian Olive trees that are impossible to ride through so you have to tie your horse up and try to get them out while on foot. If you don't have a good cow dog, it's pretty tough because they'll hang up in the brush and let you walk or crawl right past them. We ended up getting half of them in the corral at home, but those others were really tough. There was a red steer calf that was the biggest problem. I hated that calf! I would have them going where I needed them to go, then he would just take off leading all the others astray. This happened more than once. It was hunting season and the neighbors wouldn't let me on their place to get my cows back for a month. Finally we were able to go after them and got all but two cows and a calf headed downriver toward the house and corrals before it got dark. They were all there the next day but wouldn't all come in the pasture at the same time. There were always a couple that would hang back.

I was feeling pretty frustrated and on the edge of desperation. It was the end of November and our Fast Sunday was coming up. That's where we as members of our church, the Church of Jesus Christ of Latter-Day Saints, go without food and drink for a 24 hour period in fasting and prayer for the things that are important to us at the time. Sometimes, most of the time, it's a fast of thanksgiving. Other times it's for divine assistance for answers to specific things. I decided I needed divine assistance for a specific thing.... getting all my cattle gathered up.

The Thursday before Fast Sunday, I decided to get a jump on it and fasted all that day into Friday. Then I did it again Saturday noon to Sunday noon. I would throw some hay out to get the cows to come in every evening hoping to shut the gate with all of them caught, but like I said, there were always some that didn't come in with the others.

Well, one evening after feeding, they all came in. Now I needed to sneak down and shut the gate without getting caught. I almost made it. I was only about 30 yards away from the gate when they spotted me. I ran as fast as I could (*which is NOT anything to brag about!*) and beat them to it, but it was only a wire fence and I knew it wouldn't stop determined beasts like those. As I watched them charge toward the fence, I knew I was going to have a lot of fence fixing to do shortly. I quietly said to myself, "Please, don't!"

The red steer was in the lead again and just as I said that, he stopped and looked at me. So did the rest of them! I closed the gate and walked to the corral and they turned and followed me.

People who don't work with cattle wouldn't think much about this, but I know that I witnessed a miracle that evening! I was able to get good homes and prices for them after that and I didn't have to haul nearly as much hay the next summer!

Dusty

Dusty was a tough looking green-broke three year old blue roan gelding. He was a little pig-eyed which isn't all that desirable. Sometimes they can have a real attitude. He was offered to me for $500 which was a decent price for what he was at the time. He had no papers but he had good black hooves, good bones and was pretty well built. I thought I could make some money if I decided to sell him if he wasn't completely crazy. I offered $400 and took him home.

He saddled good, but when I got on him, he was really spooky like he'd been hammered on pretty hard. He never bucked with me but I was always half expecting him to. He needed something to do to keep his mind occupied so I started following calves around in a pen while riding him. He started to relax a little while doing that as opposed to flinching and trying to run away when asked to turn. It also gave him an idea what I meant when I was teaching him to neck rein. It took over ten years to finally get over the fear of getting beaten. Someone must have really been rough with him.

I took a lot of time trying not to push him too hard. He ended up turning into a top notch cow horse. When dragging calves to the branding fire, he was almost automatic. He would go just past the fire and turn the right direction, face the calf and stop. If you could catch and dally, he'd do the rest.

Eventually, he let me shoot off him. I shot several rabbits with my pistol while sitting in the saddle. He handled so well that I took him to a barrel race and placed third the first time we ever tried. There were quite a few seasoned barrel racers we competed against, too. I sure was proud of him! He really seemed to enjoy, too, but, we had ranch work to do and never made it back.

I rode him while sorting cattle and he got pretty good at that too. He must have had some Hancock in his bloodlines because not just the color, but he was tough and kind of…well, you'd better respect him. I let him in the garden spot one day so he could clean it up a little. But when I went in to catch him, he didn't want to be caught. When we finally came nose to nose, his neck was arched , nostrils flared, ears pinned back and he was ready to fight! I just stood in front of him and asked quietly, "Why are you doing this?"

I saw his eyes literally change from hard fighting mode to a soft, compliant look instantly. His formerly rigid fighting stance relaxed and he dropped his head. I haltered him then led him off without a problem.

One day I was talking to the guy who had him before me and he asked how he was doing. When I told him that we were getting along pretty well, he said that when he had him, he would walk into the pen and he never knew whether the horse was going to try to kill him or be his best friend. He asked if the horse had ever tried to buck with me and I told him that he hadn't. He said he could really buck when he wanted to. Patience is good medicine!

When he was younger, he would change color in the winter from a dark steel grey to almost white with a touch of red here and there. He was tough. He never quit on me and eventually did everything I asked him to do from gathering cattle and roping stock to packing camp or elk back to the truck.

One day I rode Ranger and Landon rode Dusty from our house to my mom's house about 50 miles away. By the time we got there, Ranger was getting tired but Dusty was still moving along pretty fresh and strong.

I miss him.

CHAPTER 9

The Bronc Ride

I was a little nervous as I climbed into the bucking chute. My bronc waited patiently as I cautiously lowered myself down onto its back, probably knowing that its' work wouldn't last too long. It was the first time I'd ever tried such a thing. I'd ridden a few horses during my short eight years of life, but they had all been gentle and broke. All I had to hang on to was a rope that was run around its chest.

"Now you hang on tight to that thing." Rosco Sizemore was good friend of the family and was offering some pretty sound advice. He was a short man with a huge bulge on his neck as a result of one too many bull riding crashes. He was fortunate that his broken neck didn't have any more serious damage than it did. He could still move around pretty freely. All except he couldn't turn his neck. He had to turn his whole body in order to look around.

Bob Broome, Clyde Slaugh and maybe another man or two were the "pickup men" in the arena. They were also friends of the family. In fact, the whole community was kind of a family when you got right down to it. They were on foot, not horseback like most other rodeos. This was the Little Buckaroo Rodeo. It was for younger kids like me. We were riding somebody's mean, spoiled or unwanted anymore Shetland ponies and calves for bucking stock.

Now, at the time, I didn't know much about riding in a rodeo. All I really knew was that you weren't supposed to get bucked off. I wanted to make my family who were watching in the stands proud of me, so I was going to follow Rosco's advice the best I could. I needed to focus all my energy on riding this wild beast until it was time to get off. Come to think of it, I'm not sure anyone bothered to tell me when that was supposed to be!

Well, it was time. The pickup men were ready, the timer was ready, and I guess Rosco and I had decided that I was ready. I don't remember if I nodded my head for them to open the gate or if I meekly vocalized it, but the chute gate opened and we were off!

At that particular time in my life, I was pretty good at following directions. I've since left that habit, attribute or whatever it's called behind me, much to the dismay of some. I had both hands choking the life out of that rope like Rosco told me to do and I wasn't letting go! My eyes were screwed shut, my arms were tight against my body, my legs were wrapped around that horse like the skin on a beaver and I WAS RIDIN'!

After the buzzer sounded, which was my cue to get off, I stayed on because I never heard it and, well you know, I WAS RIDIN'! That is when the ride got really interesting. The first pickup man grabbed at me and since my eyes were screwed shut and I'd blocked out all things except my current mission, he missed and I WAS RI…well, you know! I guess those pickup men earned their pay on that ride because they chased me and that wild horse all over the arena trying to get me off! Finally, one of them caught up with us and bodily jerked me off that pony!

Well, I didn't win, but I didn't get bucked off, either! Everybody got a kick out of it and I was proud of myself for not falling off. I remember Jack Williams got bucked off a calf and whacked his head so hard that it knocked him out. I saw his eyes roll back in his head. That was scary! He finally woke up and his eyes went back where they needed to be with the colored side out instead of the white part showing.

Did that launch a career into rodeo for me? Nope, I'm too tight to pay money to ride bucking horses when I can ride them for free at home! I used to get paid to ride them by people that didn't want to ride them themselves because I WAS RIDIN'!

CHAPTER 10

Where Do Babies Come From?

"Papa, where do babies come from?" The question came like a bolt of lightning, completely unexpected. This very same question has turned what are usually brave, fearless warriors into knock-kneed, quivering and undecided whelps; a polished, seasoned orator into a babbling fool... and my four year old grandson expected an answer... from ME!

Well, I decided I'd better give this one some thought before jumping in and explaining all the gory details. Everybody knows that kids come from God (*although I have met some that made me wonder if they came from somewhere else!*). He already knew that part, but now he was after details.

Is it a lie to maybe embellish the truth a little? Just a little, where telling a good story might get him off the subject some and get me off the hook! When does telling a good story turn into a lie, anyway? Maybe it doesn't. Maybe it's just a good ruse to get him off the subject until I can get him back to his mom. It was easier with his dad. We owned livestock and he learned pretty early what the terms, "in heat, she's in, she took, she's makin' bag," meant as well as the names for the different anatomy parts and what they were for. Yup, this was going to be interesting.

As I looked down into the trusting eyes of that little guy, I decided to... I decided to... I decided to tell him... a story. This is kind of how it went...

We had a few cows to take care of and naturally had some horses to ride too. I happened to be riding a young horse that was given different names as different events unfolded in his development into a cow horse. The name that stuck though, was Skyscraper. You'll find out why here shortly.

Anyway, he and I were going along pretty well until a killer rabbit jumped out from under a bush right next to his feet. It seemed like he was always looking for a reason to buck and this seemed like a good opportunity for him to practice his vertical leaping. He could really jump and this time he was putting all he had into it. The good thing was that he wasn't trying anything tricky, just long, pretty jumps.

"What's that got to do with babies?" Well, hang on and let me finish.

Every time he jumped, he got a little higher, until it was more like flying instead of bucking. We spent more time in the air than we did on the ground! I was starting to really enjoy the ride, although the landings were a little rough! Eventually, we got so high that I could see ol' Moroni blowing on his horn forty miles away! I wondered if I was supposed to tip my hat in respect or just keep hanging on! I chose to hang on. Now, like I said, we were scraping the sky in a way that I never imagined could happen, when suddenly I saw a flock of big white birds in front of us. It looked as though we were going to have a bird strike for sure!

Well, we missed that bunch, but on the next jump we came down right in the middle of the flock. I noticed that something was different about them, they weren't built like regular birds. Then I realized that they were storks! Each had a big sheet hanging from it's bill with something in it! We kind of landed on one of them and when that happened, we got all tangled up in the sheet.

That stork was packing a baby in the sheet! In fact, all those big ol' storks were packing babies! They must've been on their way to the hospitals to deliver all those little young people!

Well, we were in a predicament. I had to hang onto the baby so it wouldn't fall, all the while the stork and the sheet were tangled up around my head and shoulders. And to make matters worse, my horse and I had parted company and he was headed back to earth without me!

That stork had a job to do and it was to take care of that baby no matter what happened. While we were falling, the stork had finagled that sheet into a parachute! Then, it latched onto the top of the sheet and was using its big wings to slow our descent and to guide us to a good landing spot.

After we'd landed, the stork coughed up a note that had directions on it along with instructions for care and feeding. On the bottom was printed the address of the baby's new home with the parents names. The names seemed pretty familiar and I was pretty sure I knew them from somewhere... then I realized that they had the same names as my wife and I! Interesting coincidence. Or was it? Wait a minute! Was this baby supposed to be ours? I checked the address one more time. Yup, ours.

I looked at the stork for reassurance and it just squawked at me. Having never learned stork language, I was kind of at a loss for words. Now this was the first time I'd ever been this close to a stork, let alone try to have a conversation with one. About this time, the stork evidently had decided that its job was finished because it was gathering up the sheet and getting ready to leave. I started to ask what I was supposed to do when it up and flew away! No squawking or anything, it just left with me holding this little baby in my arms!

Now, I don't know how much you know about new babies, but I found out right quick that they don't come with diapers… or manners either! Needless to say, by the time I got home, we were a mess! When I looked at him, I was reminded of the biblical account of Esau's birth description," he came out all red and hairy". Well this little feller wasn't hairy, but he was sure red! (Must've gotten it from his mothers side.)

I knew from experience that newborns, whether they be calves, colts or others, need immediate nourishment and was trying to figure out how to make that happen. When I came through the front door, my wife was standing there waiting for me. She said that she'd been "expecting," (whatever she meant by that). She'd noticed that Skyscraper had returned without me and was getting ready to go hunt me down. Women are generally a lot smarter than their husbands and this relationship held true to that idea. When she saw me and the baby, she got all excited and grabbed him away from me and started nurturing him like moms are supposed to do. When I decided to give him a shot of A,D &B12, she reared up and seriously opposed the decision—kinda like trying to take a bear cub from its mother. (Maybe human babies are different from calves).

"Well Sonny, that's as close to what happened as I can recall. Since then, Skyscraper calmed down and turned into a pretty good horse and your dad grew up riding him. Ol' Skyscraper ended up being one of the best babysitters any boy ever had. I kind of like to think that he realized that he had a lot to do with bringing your dad into the family. Sorta turned into a second guardian, you might say. He took care of your dad from the first time he crawled up his leg onto his back. It seemed to be his mission in life, taking care of your dad. I think God uses animals to do some of His work."

This got me a little sentimental in telling it to my grandson, and it seemed to make an impact on him too. He keeps looking up into the sky and he just renamed his pony Ol' Cloudwalker!

PS. I had a horse named Callaway when our son Landon was growing up. This horse was all business and was one of the best horses I've ever had. I roped and caught wild cattle on him, dragged calves to the branding fire and even packed elk and camp on him. He packed me a lot of miles on fishing trips and gathering cattle. I never could get him to stand while I got on him. When Landon was pretty young, we were up on the mountain camping and I asked him if he was ready to start riding on his own. He said he was, so I told him that he could ride Callaway. I put his saddle on the horse and told him that I'd help him up after I saddled my horse.

After getting my stuff together, I turned to help Landon and saw that he was already in the saddle.

"How'd you get up there?"

"I crawled up his leg."

"What!? That horse will kick your head off!"

But he didn't. In fact, that horse wouldn't move until Landon asked him to go and yes, sometimes he'd even let Landon crawl up his leg! But, he would never wait for me! Those two were quite a team.

Callaway was the first horse he ever rode. When Callaway was a three year old, Landon was about six months old and I rode Callaway with Landon on my back in a backpack on our fishing trips. Landon would "sing" all the way up and back, unless he was asleep!

It was a terribly sad day when we had to put Callaway down due to a stroke. Sure miss him.

CHAPTER 11

Rambling and Reminiscing

Here are a few (*or more*) different things that I thought might be of interest. I'll write these out in no particular order so it really will reflect the title!

I'll start with my beginning. I was born when there were only 49 states in the USA. Hawaii was made a state in August 1959 and I was born in May that year. That means that my older siblings were born when there were only 48 states! Alaska was made a state in January 1959.

When I was growing up, these are some of the things I remember:

There was only one student in my school class who had divorced parents. Anymore, I'm scared to ask someone that I haven't seen for a while about how their spouse is doing for fear they're separated or divorced!

Besides the one above, the only single parent families I knew of were because the father had died. That was it. There were a few out of wedlock babies, but they were pretty rare and it carried a high degree of shame. Abortions were nearly unheard of. "Shacking up" was new. I remember watching a movie that featured Frankie Avalon and Annette Funicello where they talked about how in Europe people would live together to see if they got along with each other before getting married. Being an innocent little kid, I thought that was a good idea! Now I know better.

Illicit drugs were starting to be popular. All through my high school years, the ones who did drugs got beat up. Cigarette smokers and "dopers" were viewed as losers. After I graduated from high school, it was a non issue.

Just before I got old enough to go to high school, the girls were all required to wear dresses. Quite a change from today. And speaking of school, in grade school, the worst behaved kids it seemed, were children whose parents were teachers! As grade schoolers, we recited the pledge of allegiance every morning. Most of the "working mothers" were school teachers. Very few mothers worked out of the home. That was the fathers job and when his job required him to move, the family moved with him.

Playground equipment back then would make a modern day liberal have a seizure! How any of us ever survived somewhat intact will always be a mystery to them. Sure, we had accidents, but that's why there were school nurses! Most of the time, we'd rub a little dirt on the wound after we realized we were going to live, and get back on! Recess was short and precious, it couldn't be wasted by going to the nurse.

Respect for elders was expected and enforced. If we disrespected someone older than we were, we could expect swift and sure action. We got swats for most infractions in school. One of the rules when I was in Junior High was that if you forgot your gym clothes, you got five little reminders on your backside. They stung pretty well as I remember! It seemed like the "old people" were always looking for a reason to whack us and they didn't even have to be related to us to get away with it! We learned to respect others, but especially our elders.

When I was growing up, even into the late 1970's, we had what was called a party line for our phone. Two or three different households would share the same line. We each had our own number, but you had to pick the phone up and listen to make sure someone else wasn't using it. If someone was on the line, you hung up and tried later. You learned to be careful with what you said because you never knew when someone else might be listening! Most homes only had one phone in the whole house. Answering machines hadn't been invented yet so if you missed the call, you missed out. They were all rotary dial phones too. It had the piece you picked up to talk and listen with like our current phones, but it was attached to a cord that went to the phone body itself that had a wheel with numbers 1 through 0 that you would dial with. If the number you wanted to dial was 1132, you would put your finger tip in the one hole in the wheel and turn the wheel to the stop, release it and it would rotate back, then you'd do the same with the following numbers. We only had to dial the last four digits for quite a few years.

Money was hard to come by as a kid so we were always on the lookout for pop bottles. A ten or twelve ounce bottle could be redeemed for three cents while a bigger bottle brought a nickel. We thought liters were what people lit cigarettes with! Candy bars cost five and ten cents. I remember trying to decide between one ten center or two five centers several times. Some candy was two pieces for a penny.

Televisions were new when I was young and not everyone had one. Up until I was a little older, all the programs and movies were black and white. When color TV was available, you had to buy one that would show color. I remember our first color TV was a Curtis Mathis. It was in a big wooden cabinet. My dad was pretty proud of it! There were three networks, ABC, NBC & CBS. They all signed off with the national anthem at midnight. We got three TV stations from Salt Lake City. I remember Bob Welty was the weather man and Dick Norse covered sports with Shelly Thomas filling us in on the news. They had what they called "The Big Money Movie" every afternoon. During the course of the movie they'd have a break when the host would open the phone book, pick out a number and call to see if they were watching. If they were and could answer the question asked, they won some money. I think every wrong answer or when no one answered the phone, the money pot grew $10. We didn't have video movies, we had film movie cameras with reels that took home movies without sound that needed a projector to project the picture onto a screen. Every now and then, the film would break and Dad would have to splice it back together so we could finish the reel. After it was over, it would need rewound like the VCR tapes that are now obsolete. There were the eight track tapes that were the predecessors of cassette tapes too. Seemed like everybody had a stack of them in their home and truck! Vinyl records were the best sound you could get. They were still popular in the early '80s, but got replaced by CD's along with the cassette tapes.

Restaurants were for special occasions. No one I knew "ate out" very regularly. I can probably count on one hand the number of times our family ate at a restaurant together. Then there was what is today called "Ethnic Food". Pizza and Mexican food were uncommon. I remember when the roller skating rink had a pizzeria in it. It was a big deal! None of the local restaurants served Mexican food until later.

There were ash trays in nearly every business you went into as a courtesy for the cigarette smokers. When you went into a café or restaurant you got a good charge of smoke first thing. I hated it. It's a lot better now.

The first microwave oven I ever saw or even knew about was owned by my aunt in Idaho Falls. That was 1979 I think. It was magic! I was going to college in Rexburg, Idaho, 25 miles away.

One afternoon I'd been visiting some girls in our college ward and when I got to my truck, someone had left a bag in the back behind the cab. In it was a knitted two-tone green afghan . I was really concerned that someone had lost it. I couldn't imagine someone doing all that work just to give to me! I asked all around trying to find the rightful owner to no avail. I eventually decided that maybe it was put there on purpose. I still have it and never did find out where it came from.

I remember the first 500cc motorcycle I ever saw . It was a Kawasaki 500 street bike. It was the biggest I'd ever seen with the exception of Blaine Murrays Harley. Stock racks in the back of pickup trucks and two ton stock trucks were common then. There weren't the big stock trailers like there are now. All pickups had manual locking hubs until the early '70s. Most had manual transmissions too. There weren't diesel engines in pickups either.

Some of the high school kids had their own vehicle, but most families had one or two family cars. It was seldom for a kid to be given a car for their 16th birthday. Some of the guys would work on the oil rigs during the summer and had some money to spend along with their new truck. If you wanted it, you earned it. Good practice to live by.

Tattoos. The only people that had them were some of the men who had served in the armed forces. No one could imagine a girl or woman ever having one. Most men didn't have any and those that did, often tried to cover them if possible as they got older.

Hunting season was a big deal since there was only one rifle deer season and one rifle elk season. They alternated every other year which one started first, and they were 9 days long. If you were after elk, you had to travel up above Meeker or other high country because there weren't any down lower. Deer were plentiful in the lower country. That started to change in the late '80s. Elk kind of replaced the deer everywhere.

My first elk hunting trip was when I was 12 years old. Dad decided to take me with him on Milk Creek where he grew up. The opening day was warm and sunny but that night it snowed about a foot. We stayed in a small wall tent with what he called a sheepherder wood stove. It saved the trip. I had boots that leaked so I had about four pairs of socks on to try to keep my feet from getting too cold. Forget about warm! I remember melting some together while holding my cold feet up to the stove. He'd just gotten new glasses and as we hiked around, they fogged up on him quite a bit when he stopped. We finally found some elk and one was a bull, but every time he shouldered his rifle his glasses fogged up! He shot and wounded the bull but then lost him because of his foggy glasses. I kept telling him where the elk went and eventually, we got him. He told me that that was the first and maybe only elk he ever killed with someone with him. I was glad it was me!

On the way up the horse kicked the wooden side out of the trailer, fell out and got drug down the gravel road ¼ mile. All his ribs on one side were visible but he lived through it. A couple years later all that was left was a small three or four inch scar. He's the one that Mom was riding that drowned while crossing the river.

Dad used to watch his dad's sheep when he was a kid. He would tie a quart jar of cream in his slicker behind his saddle in the morning and by the end of the day, it would be butter!

....

Back then it wasn't that unusual to see outhouses still in use. In fact, when we got married, we had no indoor plumbing but we had a nice "modern" steel outhouse! We used it for nearly a year while we were building our house. Sure got cold in the winter when it was -35°F! It's behind my shop now. It's equipped with wet wipes and a battery powered light along with toilet paper! Stylin'!

Outhouses in the old days would sometimes blow up with people in them. Usually men. It was common for a regularly used outhouse to be kind of odorous. Part of the odor was the methane that's released by the sewage breaking down. It was decided that when the men sat down to do their business, that they'd light up a cigarette and that would ignite the methane and cause the explosion. We know now what's called the fire triangle. For a fire or ignition, you need three things; oxygen, fuel and heat or an ignition source. When these guys lit one up, they, in-turn, got lit up!

Now since most of these incidents happened in the southwest, I have another theory. They cook with lots of hot peppers in that part of the country. I've eaten some pretty spicy food, but nothing like what is on their regular diet so I can only imagine how they feel while doing their business! There have been times that I felt akin to the space shuttle liftoff myself! Maybe some of those explosions didn't involve cigarettes after all!

....

People back then could and did bottle their own brew. My wife tells about how she and her siblings would scour the country for discarded beer bottles. Her mom would then clean them up while her dad mixed all the ingredients together. When it was ready, they would fill the bottles and they had a bottle capper to cap the bottles with. The kids loved to tip back a bottle when someone was driving by and watch the rubber necking double take! Rex made some pretty good root beer! Pam said that they were drinking their root beer from the beer bottles on a camping trip when a lady asked them what they were drinking. "Root beer!" was the enthusiastic reply. She asked if she could have some too! Maybe she wanted to make sure that that was all they were drinking!

....

When I was about 17 years old, one of our youth leaders was a recently returned missionary. We were playing in the gym when I felt the need to use the restroom. A younger 12 year old went in before me and another boy a little younger than me followed. I don't think I was ever mean, but I did like to joke around with people. We sat the 12 year old up on the sink counter when another leader came in and demanded to know what we were doing. The little guy saw his chance for an escape and took it. The rest of us ended up in what I thought was a playful scuffle that ended up with the leader getting a lot more serious than we ever would have. Later on, I was back in the gym when I playfully shadow boxed the returned missionary leader. I never touched him but he slapped me on the side of my head...hard! He looked at me like he wanted to fight! I thought that his mission must not have done him any good or he wouldn't have done that! He was several years older and a lot bigger. I was shocked at what he did. He had no reason that I knew of to do that and he never told me why. I'd just gotten beat on by two men who were supposed to be trusted leaders. I didn't ever want to have anything to do with them or the Church if that was who and what they were. When my mom came and picked me up to take me home she asked how things went and I told her that I never wanted to go back to those people or that church.

I worked with another returned missionary on the cow outfit. He was always trying to talk me into going on a mission. He was another poor example to me. "Do as I say, not as I do", kind of guy. I won't give any specific examples but he didn't keep the promises he made in the temple. Not even close. It didn't look to me like that mission did him any good either. Add to those, two of my roommates in college who were terrible examples and you can maybe understand why I didn't want to be associated with any of those kind of people. No mission for me.

I'd always respected those who had returned from missions, even almost revered them to a point, but these guys were a serious trial for me. Deep inside I knew I was just using them as an excuse not to do what I knew I needed to do. I knew that I needed to answer for the things I did and not let other peoples' poor examples keep me from doing what I needed to do.

Those others have their own problems to deal with and they'll be judged accordingly. I have enough problems of my own without trying to pack theirs too. Thanks to some curious circumstances, I did end up going on and serving a mission and have been incredibly blessed ever since. The first two leaders mentioned, ended up being my bishops later on. The cowboy married and moved to a different town. He also ended up as a bishop. I guess there is such a thing as repentance and forgiveness.

....

As a kid, I remembered Christmas as a magical time. The stores didn't seem to start their Christmas advertising until after Thanksgiving, which as far as I'm concerned, is how it should be. Anyway, I remember getting a silver dollar to spend on gifts for my siblings. I remember going into the Ben Franklin store in Vernal on main street to do a lot of my shopping. There was always popcorn popping in there and the smells of Christmas. The cashier ladies were always friendly and "Merry Christmas" was heard everywhere, even to us little kids after we made our purchases. It was serious business, shopping and keeping our gifts hidden from our siblings!

After we got home, each of us would take our turn in our parents bedroom to wrap our presents alone. Secrecy was so thick, it permeated the whole house. After wrapping the gifts, we would carry them into the living room where the tree was at and stash them under the tree while looking for any others that had our name on them. Then we had to wait until Christmas to open them. Anticipation was pretty heavy!

Every year we would get what came to be known as the "Wish Book" in the mail. It was the Christmas catalog from Montgomery Wards. It was about an inch and a quarter thick and had about anything a kid could want in it.

By the time Christmas showed up, it was in tatters. The pages were marked, wrinkled and torn from five little kids "wishing" while looking at it for the previous month. I remember asking Santa Clause for a BB gun one year. I got a plastic toy gun instead. I was pretty sure he didn't hear me right and must have thought I said Baby gun!

Christmas Eve was crazy! I remember watching the TV news from Salt Lake and waiting for the Santa report to make sure he was on his way! There was a little cut-out on the screen of Santa and his reindeer going across the sky. He's coming! He's on his way! I remember hearing and seeing my dad chuckle when the news guys said that there was something coming our way from the North Pole. This was no laughing matter! Santa was on his way and he was coming to our house that very night! There was no way we were getting any sleep that night! Dad lined us all up after evening prayers and gave each of us a dose of Nyquil to help us calm down. It lasted until about 4am. Our house had hardwood floors that creaked a lot. All of us kids slept in the same room and one of the older kids would try to sneak past Mom and Dads room to peak at what Santa had brought.

"Get back to bed!" squeak, squeak, squeak, squeak! A little later the floor told on us again. "Get back to bed!" squeak, squeak, squeak, squeak…We finally wore Dad down enough that he realized that no one was getting any more sleep for quite a while. Certainly not until after all the gifts were opened.

Then there were the smells of Christmas. The turkey that was cooking in the oven all night, the aroma of pies, cranberry stuffing and peppermint candy. The smell of the pine tree. It was great!

Breakfast consisted of those little boxes of cereal that came in a variety pack. Each one was a small serving and they were made to open from the front with the box laying down. We opened the box along the perforations and then slit open the wax paper to get to the cereal. Then we would just pour the milk into the box on the cereal.

Music was everywhere during the season. In Vernal, there would be chime bells playing Christmas carols on main street, all the shops and stores had music playing and we would play Christmas music at home on the record player. In school we would sing carols and everyone enthusiastically participated.

For several years, Santa would bring me a new pair of cowboy boots. Once, he even filled one of them up with the hard candy that we always got for Christmas. We always got an orange in our stocking in addition to the hard candy.

He brought us a wooden toboggan one year. We used to get a lot of snow back then. We used it a lot! One year, Grandma came for a couple days. She's Dad's mom and the only grandma we had as Mom's mom passed away just after my older brother was born. I remember asking if she saw Santa when he came Christmas Eve and she said that she did! Wow! What an experience! Nobody ever saw him, but she did! I was more than impressed! She slept on our couch by the Christmas tree, but said she stayed really still so he would think that she was still sleeping!

....

Four letter words were not spoken in public. They were especially forbidden on TV and radio. None of the music had them either. Sure is different now that the world is becoming more "enlightened". I had to turn my radio down the other day to avoid hearing some commonly used bad language. A coworker of mine and someone who knows better is the worst offender in our office. I sure get disappointed in people. I'm not saying that I'm innocent of any of it, but I certainly don't use that language in my everyday conversations like most everyone else seems to. I'm doing a lot better since we got rid of the cows! Jon Hill's grandpa told him that to be a cowboy, you had to have a horse and know how to cuss! Jon said that he could count on one hand the times he heard his other grandpa cuss. Both were top notch cowboys, they just had different philosophies.

....

There is a pretty good sized drainage called Cottonwood Wash that we needed to cross in order to get to the ranch house and corrals. It didn't have a bridge crossing it so you had to drive across the wash itself. It was generally dry most of the time, but in the summer time it might rain miles away and not at the ranch, but you still needed to watch out for flash floods.

I was about 12 years old when my younger sister, her younger friend and I were across the wash from the house. It had rained and the ground was wet but not too muddy. It was in the late afternoon and I heard a rumble that didn't sound right.

I trotted up the bank next to the wash to check and sure enough, I could see a wall of water coming down the wash. I hollered at the girls to come running. We had enough time to make it across before the water got to where we were. I could have made it alone but felt like I needed to take care of the girls. Well, they didn't hurry and by the time they showed up, the water was several feet deep and raging. There was no way we were making it across until the water dropped and that could take several hours.

It was getting along toward evening and starting to get dark when I knew we were going to have to spend the night in the tamarack patch. The water was still running high and loud when Mom showed up with a sleeping bag. She gave it a mighty throw and it only got a little wet when the end of it landed at the edge of the water. I only remember one bag, but there may have been two. Anyway, we spent the night in the brush because somebody wouldn't listen. I was pretty disgusted.

....

I watched my younger sister get scalped one day. She had long, blonde hair and was next to the air compressor while it was running. As she bent down for something, her hair got caught in the drive belt that connected the motor to the compressor. It jerked her nearly off her feet but she was able to keep from getting pulled all the way into the pulley. She actually stalled it out! That was a strong motor, but she was stronger! She had a bloody patch on her head where some of her hair was ripped out, but it grew back! Scary! She's pretty tough!

CHAPTER 12

The Throw

It was the last day of school and it was a time to celebrate! As was the custom, we gathered up a bunch of water balloons and wandered around town searching for one of our buddies or....an opportunistic target to show itself.

Glen was a nice, quiet, well-behaved young man and we got along pretty well together. He just happened to be my partner in crime for the day. We were on Main Street when he made "The Throw". Now, I've made a couple throws myself that I'm pretty proud of. One in particular happened after "The Throw," but it was probably my best.

We were seniors in high school during Building Trades class. Every year the school Building Trades class worked on building a house. We had lots of fun in that class in addition to learning some pretty important life skills, like don't stand in a water puddle while plugging in a circular saw. Freaky was kind enough to teach us that lesson one day after a rainstorm. As he vibrated around doing the "electric man dance," we were all pretty impressed with his athleticism! And no, getting shocked doesn't frizz your hair like some would have you believe!

Anyway, back to my throw. We got a fresh blanket of nice, wet snow overnight and, being high school kids, we were determined to sample its packing qualities. After trying it out for distance throwing, we decided it to be our duty to try it out for accuracy as well. We just had to find a suitable target. Terry. He was a natural target. Underclassman with a cocky attitude. He was bigger than me by quite a bit and probably the same age, but back then, if you didn't make the grade, you got to try again the next year. So, he was hiding behind this power pole laughing at our poor marksmanship while feeling pretty safe. After a miss he would stick his face out from behind the pole and make fun of us. Like I said, the snow was as good as it gets for making snowballs. In fact, it was so wet that if you packed it enough, water would drip out of your fingers making it almost an ice ball rather than a snowball. I happened to have a high quality, drippy projectile like that in my chilly right hand.

Great moments are often a combination of very favorable circumstances that happen to all line up at the same time. This was one of those situations; the right snowball, the right target, the right timing, and of course the right throw with all the velocity I could muster.

As was mentioned earlier, Terry was giving us quite a bit of harassment due to poor accuracy and/or timing. All of that was about to come to a very abrupt stop. I wound up and tried to time it just right, and as he poked his head around the pole, my snowball drilled him right in the middle of the forehead leaving a bright red mark at the point of impact. He stopped laughing but the others didn't!

Isn't it interesting how seemingly small things like a snowball can change someone's mood so suddenly? For some reason, after that, everyone stopped throwing snowballs at him. I guess they were just in awe of finally actually being present and witnessing what had to be the perfect throw! Their respect and reverence for the occasion was hard to notice right then because Terry was jealous that he couldn't make a throw like that! In fact, he was highly upset and it took quite a while to get him calmed down.

That was a great throw along with a fair amount of drama, but Glen's throw had even more than that! As was mentioned earlier, we were walking down Main Street, each of us carrying at least one full water balloon looking for any target that might avail itself. It was a beautiful day; warm and sunny. Back then air conditioning in vehicles was still kind of a luxury so most people drove around with their windows rolled down when it was warm or hot outside.

That happened to be the case when the next target showed up. This car came by and Glen lobbed a water balloon at it hitting the door post just in front of the rolled down window. At times, I am completely amazed at the quick reaction time some people exhibit in epoch moments like these! The woman driver slammed on the brakes, jammed it in park and opened the door in less time than it took for Glen's balloon to leave his hand, hit the car and cool down what was an obviously overheated woman.

Glen's thoughtful act of helping this overheated individual to lower the temperature in her car didn't seem to be met with any appreciation whatsoever! When she came boiling out of that car with her hair all wet and stringy and her cigarette stuck to her shirt, I could immediately sense that she wasn't getting out to thank him for cooling her off or to congratulate him on such a great throw. No, like Terry she refused to recognize the majesty of the moment. Maybe that was her last cigarette, maybe she was on her way to show her husband her new hairstyle, who knows! What I was noticing what appeared to be someone in a highly agitated state of mind and quickly decided that I didn't need that much negativity ruining my beautiful day, so I left. I didn't look back. (*Kind of like running from a grizzly bear, you just have to outrun your buddy.*)

Well, she caught him. She wasn't content to just tell him how unhappy she was. No, she and he took a trip to the cop shop where she expressed her displeasure of Glen's thoughtfulness to all who would listen to her. They consoled her enough that she finally went on her way, convinced that she'd done her part to make the world a better place by eliminating one more criminal from the streets and leaving Glen in the custody of Rangely's finest. They waited until she was gone, then just told him to not do it any more and turned him loose.

So what makes this worthy of "The Throw"? The drama. There may have been better throws somewhere but few equal the circumstances and drama that this one had. I still chuckle to myself when I remember the arc of the balloon, the impact, the drenching of the car and woman, the sudden stop with this mad, stringy haired demon blowing out of the car with the cigarette stuck to her shirt! The cigarette. It just seems to cap it all off.

I can't tell you anything about the car or who the woman was, but I remember the stringy dark hair and the cigarette, right in front of where the drug store used to be on the corner of Main Street and White Avenue.

CHAPTER 13

Lookin' Fer A Wife

Are you the guy to talk to about buyin' an ad in the newspaper?

Yeah, I do. I'm not sellin' anythin'; I want to put a Want ad in your paper. What am I lookin' fer? A, a wife. Yup, I would like to place an ad fer a wife. Fer me! Not fer somebody else! I don't want somebody else's problem, er wife. I want my own! I'm not into sharin'. Call me selfish if ya want to, but it won't make no difference. I'm ready to settle down and experience the joys of heavenly matrimony and marital bliss that I keep hearin' about.

Characteristics? What do ya mean? Some people claim that I'm a characteristic. Is that what ya mean?

Oh! Physical characteristics. Yeah, she needs to be humanly female with all the standard features—two arms, two legs, a head on top of her neck and shoulders, original plumbing—not altered, and most, if not all of her teeth. She'll need those fer makin' buckskin. The thing about that is, after she's chewed on several hides to soften 'em up, her jaws'll be stout enough to bite your fingers off so she needs to be good natured, too.

Have I ever been married before? Well kinda—I think. Well, there was a gal that stayed with me fer a while—at least I think she was a gal. We never kissed each other, so I don't think it was really constipated.

What? Consummated? Same thing, ain't it? Anyway, I don't think we was ever officially married. Never was really sure about that. Not really even sure if she was completely human either.

Well, she was kinda skittish about closed places like cabins and such. Never would come inside. Always stayed outside, even in the cold and when it was stormin'. She would just scratch a hole in the dirt and curl up under a bush or a tree.

Oh! That reminds me. She has to get along with my dog. This other gal didn't like my dog and he got to where he was purty skeered of her!

Well, she bit him. I thought I was gonna lose him there for a while, but he pulled through. He stayed away from her after that.

Why'd she bite him? Well, you know how when you find an old buff'ler or elk carcass that's been there quite a while and has ripened up really good, how dogs and such like to roll on 'em and get all perfumed up? Well, he rolled on her one too many times and she got tired of it, so she bit him. Prob'ly didn't help when he squirted her those other times, either.

When I suggested she take a bath, she got a little defensive. Then I happened to mention that maybe she was skeered of soap and water. She claimed that she warn't skeered of soap and water, just as long as they warn't mixed. She brought tears to the eyes of all who met her! Maybe that's why she stayed out of closed places!

It would be nice if the prospect could cook too. I'd been gone on my trap line for a couple weeks and got back to find that this gal had cooked up a batch of stew. I checked to make sure my dog was still alive before I tried any! Can't take any chances!

Ya know, it's not always good manners to ask what yer a bein' fed, so I ladled up a cup and tried some. It warn't too bad! In fact it tasted fairly palatable! I wanted to encourage her with her cookin' efforts so I tried to think of a compliment that would serve that purpose.

Generally, stew gets better with age if'n ya throw some stuff in to make up fer what ya took out every day. If'n ya cover it up an' keep it cool over-night, it'll last quite a while.

I didn't remember havin' any rice stocked up, so I asked her where she got the rice that was in the stew. She said that she didn't put any rice in the stew. It looked like rice. It was shaped like rice. Same color an' size as rice. IT WASN'T RICE! Suddenly, for some reason I felt as full as I could be. In fact, I was so full that I was just about to run over! I didn't eat any more of that stew. Shortly after that, she wandered off and I never saw her again. I guess that means that our relationship is over.

So, back to the ad. Other characteristics? Well, she needs to be old enough to be a woman and young enough to do the work.

As far as looks go, I'm not too particular—just as long as she doesn't' scare my dog away. She'd have to be pretty hideous for that to happen. It would be nice if she would keep her hair tied or done up so's she wouldn't be draggin' it through the food.

Maybe… maybe for special occasions, she could put a dab of bacon grease behind each ear heh, heh, heh! Maybe even some on, on her mouth!
Ooooweee!! I'm getting' myself all worked up and excited! I gotta calm down! I don't know how much more of this Marital Bliss I can handle and I ain't even married yet! Whew!

Kids? I guess she could bring them along if she has some. I kinda prefer eatin' elk and buffler. I'm not much into eating goat meat. Oh! Children kind of kids! I'm with ya now. Well I guess it'd depend on the situation and how noisy they are. I don't like noisy.

What're some of my characteristics? Wall, just sit down there and let me tell ya!

I use rattlesnake fangs for toothpicks!

I ride thunderbolts for fun!

The Cheyenne, Shawnee an' Blackfoot run fer cover when they see me a comin'!

I cook my meat with lightnin' an' season it with brimstone!

I have "corn rows" braided into my chest hair!

I'm a Man's man in a compact loveable package!

But I am a might squeamish around spiders and stink bugs! Repulsive critters! Just repulsive!

Contact information? Just send it to the post office tree in Browns Park in care of Butch Cavity. I stop by there every month or so. Thanks a bunch! I'll be in touch.

CHAPTER 14

The Bear Man

Back in '26, I was trappin' beaver in the country now known as Pikes Peak. I was a "free trapper" and doin' as well or better 'n most of the other trappers that I knew of. The thing about being a free trapper as opposed to bein' a part of a comp'ny was that my partner and I got to keep everthin' we caught. We warn't tied up to anybody else. That in itself brought on its own bag of troubles.

Because we were fewer, we were easier targets for any critter that felt a need for anythin' we had, whether it be horses, plunder or even scalps. I can do without the first two, albeit not easily, but me and my scalp, we been together since before that midwife drug me out 'n the cold and slapped me! We're purty close and I'd hate for that to change.

Horses? They make noise and tracks. Takes a heap of watchin' to keep 'em, too. Seems like there's always somebody out prowlin' around lookin' for another horse. We need horses to pack our gear 'n plews as well as ourselves. Not that we're too lazy to walk, they just come in purty handy when somebody comes after you a wantin' to poke you full of holes and give you a closer shave than you really care for. Yup, horses are worth the trouble they bring.

Speakin' of lazy, that brings me to the original intent of this story. Frank Linus Beauregard Alfonso Hezikiah Taylor. Long name, I know, but his folks had six daughters and him. Not 'zactly what his pa had planned. He wanted five sons and since he only got one, he loaded him down with the names he'd planned for all the other sons he never got. At least it's not as long as some of the Spanish names I know of. They can start telling you their full name on Sunday morning and you can come back Wednesday afternoon and catch the end of it. Anyway, we just called him Frank. The Utes called him somethin'

I can't pronounce, but it translates into something like Winter Bear because he was so oversized that he looked like a bear gettin' ready to hibernate.

Frank was the original conservative—at least when it came to expendin' —or in his words wastin', energy. The only time he showed a hankerin' for motion was when there was food to eat. He took a great amount of pride in his ability to pack his paunch with more food than six hungry men could. If there was bread a cookin', you'd best stand back. He guarded it like it was the lost Spanish hoard and he still had most of his teeth and warn't a'skeered to use 'em on anythin'!

Like I said, he was a large feller. It took half a dozen buckskins to make a buckskin shirt for him. If'n his belt warn't so wide, you could use it for a lash rope on a pack animal. Surprisingly, he got around fairly well when he had to. How in the world he got it into his head to be a mountain man is a mystery no one will ever know in this lifetime. But, here he was, ol' Sasquatch himself dressed in stretchy new buckskins. No, he warn't my partner, but I knew him personally and all knew of his propensity for gluttony. Poor ole Shingles found out the hard way.

Frank was guardin' some biscuits that the camp cook was pulling out of the coals when Shingles up and grabbed a couple before Frank or the cook could stop him. Problem was that Frank always considered the first batch as his own and he warn't about to allow such brazen thievery on his watch. Frank bellered at him as Shingles stuffed one in his mouth and as he tried to make his getaway, he tripped over a cookin' pot on the ground. Unfortunately, Frank was right behind him and tripped on the same pot. Frank fell on him and that was the end of poor ole Shingles. Squashed him like a bug.

While they were still in camp, some Utes came in wantin' to do some tradin'. One old warrior looked like he'd helped Noah herd the animals onto the ark. He looked old and he WAS old. There was a story going around that, when he was young, he'd spent a winter in a bear's den with a live bear still in it! Now, I've heard some pretty good tales in my time and some might even have a little bit of truth sprinkled in here and there, but this was one story I had to hear from the source for myself. An' here was my chance.

Now these Utes woulda been the best poker players that ever dusted an ace if they ever learned how to play. Their expression never changed an' you couldn't tell if what they told you would save your life or ruin it just so's they could get the credit for it. So, after he was asked about the story, we warn't sure he'd heard us 'cause he just looked at us for a couple minutes without changin' expressions or answerin'. I kinda wonder if he was thinkin' of how to juice it up a little. Then he nodded his head that we took for a "yes," sat down on the dirt an' told us all about it.

Seems like he was tryin' to put up a little more meat before the winter got too much further along. He'd kilt an elk an' was cuttin' it up so's he could bring it back to camp, when a pack of wolves came after 'im. He got away, but as he was runnin' through the snow, he caught his leg between a couple logs that were covered with snow an' broke it just above the ankle. He was in some serious trouble an' knew he couldn't make it back to his lodge without freezin' to death or gettin' finished off by the wolves. He had to find somethin' to make a splint out of so he started lookin' for some branches or saplin's. As he asked the Great Spirit for guidance, he felt impressed to go to a big pile of logs an' branches. If you've ever been in down timber, you'll know what he was talkin' about. As he was draggin' himself through the snow, he fell into a deep, dark hole next to that pile.

Tryin' to get his bearin's, he looked around an' found that he was layin' right next to a huge grizzly bear! Thankfully, it was still sleepin'! Again, he prayed to the Great Spirit and felt impressed to kiss the bears nose. After he did that, he got so sleepy so quick that the next thing he knew, he was snuggled up to the bear and was fallin' asleep.

When he woke up, the snow was meltin' and his leg was pretty much healed. He'd been sleepin' a whole month or more as we know time, an' warn't nothin' but skin 'n' bones. A walkin' skeleton, you might say. A mighty hungry skeleton at that. Took him a couple days to get back to his lodge an' nearly scared the tribe clean out of the country! They figured he was dead. Jus' about, but not quite. Made a purty good story but like I said, I was a thinkin' he might've embellished it just a scoach.

My partner an' I took off for the high country a little after that to gather up some more beaver pelts before we got snowed in. We did toler'ble well an' settled in with Broken Nose an' his Cheyenne band to wait out the winter. We wintered well an' the snow was meltin' purty good an' the grass was thinkin' of doin' a little growin', when, on a cool an' mostly cloudy afternoon we saw it. A dark speck in the sky an' it was a comin' our way. We couldn't figure out what it was an' the closer it got, the more befuddled we got.

It warn't shaped like a bird. In fact, we didn't rightly know what it was shaped like as far as critters go. Jus' kinda a big--really big--square thing glidin' toward us. Didn't flap its wings or nothin', just glided along.

The whole village was a watchin' this thing a comin' our way with a great deal of interest. The braves started stringin' their bows when it looked like it planned on landin' in our camp. Squaws started to chatter to the 'pooses and herdin' 'em towards the bushes by the stream while glancin' up at what ever'body had decided was the Demon of Death.

You see, some Christian missionaries had done some preachin' to 'em a few years earlier and had done their level best to convert 'em from their pagan and wicked ways. They told 'em that if they didn't change their ways, they'd be given to the demons in hell forever. Looked to them like their reckonin' was on its way.

The closer it got, the louder an' more intense the shrieking from the squaws became. All that accomplished was to encourage the 'pooses to shriek an' holler too. Of course the dogs couldn't be left out an' they was a carryin' on with as much gusto in this crazy melee as the tribe was.

About this time the critter was close enough that some of the braves turned a few arrows loose at it. Must've made it mad 'cause that's when the real bedlam started. That critter ripped out a scream that made every hair in camp stand on end!

My partner was just a few years from his Irish homeland an' had forgotten to leave some of his beliefs an' traditions back there where they belonged. He still believed in Banshees, whatever they are. He screamed out, "Banshee!"—an' took off like a cat with turpentine under its tail! Next thing I know, everybody's a runnin' 'round screamin' "Banshee! Banshee!" an' they didn't know any better than I did what a banshee was, but it must've been a banshee, 'cause that's what ever'body was a callin' it!

The closer it got, the more hair raisin' its screeches got until even the bravest of the braves were droppin' their bows an' arrows an' headin' for the brush. I'd a been in towards the front if'n one of them barkin' dogs wouldn't of tried to gnaw my leg off between barkin' an' howlin'. Guess it was jes' excited to finally meet a banshee. Now, I'll prob'ly get the hydrophoby. Hope not.

By the time I was about to get to safety, I looked back one more time. Here come that screamin' thing about a hunnert miles an hour. It smacked into one tipi, bounced off another an' another an' another until it finally landed. Each time it hit a tipi, it would make a noise that even made the dogs take off a runnin' the other way.

Now I've seen some graceful landings in my time an' this warn't one of 'em. It got me curious enough to stop an' watch. Sometimes I'm more curious than brave or smart and it's caused me grief. I wondered if this would end up being the last time I got that luxury.

Like I said, the landing was less than graceful. In fact, it was more of a flop on the ground than anythin'. No landin' gear stuck out or nothin'. It lay there for what seemed to be a few minutes before it groaned an' moved again. Slowly it raised up. It had a shaggy, dark head an' the body had shorter dark hair, an' some places it didn't seem to have much hair at all.

Its head moved around a while until it seemed to focus on me. I was a wonderin' if banshees or whatever this thing was could be kilt with a huntin' knife—or if they could be kilt at all—when it made some more sounds, not screachin', but almost sounded human. Prob'ly a banshee trick an' I warn't havin' none of it. Then, I swear it called my name! Now I knew I was in trouble! This devil demon, banshee or whatever it was had come for me an' I didn't want to go!

I pulled out my knife an' hadn't decided which way to run—I was goin' to run somewhere –when it called my name again. Now I couldn't run at all because my knees an' legs were as wobbly as a newborn buffler calf. I couldn't go anywhere! I was doomed.

It saw its chance an' started toward me. Not fast, actually kinda slow like it was a stalkin' me. I reached down deep an' found a spoonful of courage an' stood up to face my fate. If I was a gonna die, I'd do it with honor! But I'd still be dead. With a thousand beady eyes watchin' from the brush, I held my ground. I could hear some squaws singin' the Cheyenne death song an' I wondered if it was for me.

As it got closer. it seemed to take on kind of a human form. Then it spoke my name again. I could see the pearly gates startin' to open in my mind an' braced myself for the attack that I knew was about to come. The death chant became even louder an' more intense which didn't do much for my state of mind.

"Do you have anythin' to eat?"

"Wha...What?!" I coulda swore it asked for somethin' to eat! I thought that I was going to be whatever it was that was going to be served up.

"Got any grub?"

"Huh?! Grub?"

I couldn't answer for the shock an' relief that came over me was like a wave of new life. It didn't want to eat me after all! By this time it was close enough that I recognized that it was a man. It looked like he kinda had a blanket wrapped around him, but it didn't look quite right.

About now, the Indians were startin' to venture out of their hidin' places but still keepin' their distance.

"Who ARE you?

"I'm Frank."

"Frank?

"Yup."

"I didn't know what you were. How long you been flyin'?"

"Jus' today. It's a long story. Got any grub? I'll tell you while I eat."

By now I could tell that he didn't have a blanket at all, jus' lots of loose skin. He was so hairy that it jus' looked like he had a blanket on. We got him an elk hide to wrap up in. He seemed a might chilled from his flight.

Well, if you thought that ole Utes story was a whopper, jus' wait'll you hear this'n. Cinch'er down n hang on 'cause here it comes!

Somehow Frank talked his way into gettin' some comp'ny trappers to let 'im come with 'em by promisin' to do his fair share. They were purty reluctant, but he badgered 'em enough that they agreed to let 'im come. That was one decision they regretted in a hurry. They'd planned on winterin' out up there in the high mountains so's they could catch some prime sable, wolf and cats. After a month with Frank around, they nearly ran out of food.

One night they cooked up an extra big meal an' celebrated by draggin' out a jug o' whiskey. They were goin' after a big Griz bear they'd tracked to his den earlier that week and were celebratin' in advance. Like always, Frank slicked down his share of grub and then some. Then he proceeded to guzzle half the whiskey before they could get it away from him. He covered up in his lean-to all snug an' warm then went right to sleep. When he woke up, it was snowin' an' snowin' hard. While he was sleepin', the others had pulled up camp an' left him. Alone. No food.

There warn't no tracks 'cause the snow had filled them in an he warn't much of a tracker, anyhow. He was in trouble an' he knew it. He had to have shelter an' food, lots of it. Or, he could try to find his way off the mountain. Purty dangerous in a snowstorm. Too many ways to get lost an' die.

He could build up his shelter, but he still needed food. Then he thought of the griz bear. Even a big one would only last him a couple weeks, if that, the way he ate. The griz was his only chance for survival so he headed for the den. It was late in the day when he finally found it. The griz hadn't been in there very long and he wondered if it was sleepin' yet. How long does it take for a griz to get to sleep, anyway? An hour, a day, a week? Do they sleep an' then wake up before they get serious about hibernatin'?

He didn't have much time before it got too dark to see, so he tried to slip in quiet and easy so's he could shoot him without wakin' him up. It was a purty tight squeeze, an' he barely made it in far enough that he could make out part of the bear. It was sleepin', but was what he could see the front end or the back end? It was purty dark an' he couldn't tell very well. He thought he could see the head resting on the front paws so he snuck the rifle barrel up, cocked the hammer and pulled the trigger. A deafenin' CLICK scared him worse than if the gun had gone off!

The griz never even twitched. One more time. CLICK! Wet powder won't burn. He tried to back out but the sticks and branches were pointed the wrong way and kept hangin' him up. He tried to turn around but it was too tight. He couldn't even work his possibles bag, powder horn or anythin' else off his shoulders. He was trapped in a den with a sleepin' grizzly an' no way out! He surely was in a sticky wicket.

The air was gettin' purty close an' thin. He was doin his best to fight the panic that was wellin' up inside him. He knew that if the panic beat him, so would the griz. The thought of being the last midnight snack before hibernatin' started wasn't sittin' too well with 'im. He had to figure somethin' out an' quick! Somethin' that would free him up without wakin' up the griz. Then it came to him. The story about the old Ute warrior that claimed to have hibernated with a bear. Now what was it that he said he did that made him sleep for a month? Somethin' peculiar… what WAS it! If he couldn't remember, he could kiss his life adios.

Kiss! That was it! He had to kiss the bear! Now, how does one proceed with the osculation process with a bear? Is it different for sows as opposed to boars? He certainly didn't want to offend it, but he sure didn't want to try to check to see which he was dealin' with, either. Prob'ly didn't make any difference. Or did it?

Do you pucker up? He was purty puckered right now anyway, but not the kissin' kind of pucker. Do you stick out your tongue like a dog? Or do you just settle down for some good ole fashioned smoochin? Jus' the thought made his stomach sick, an' when your stomach is as big as his, that's a lot of misery!

Well, it was do or die time. Never did like that sayin', 'specially now! He wiped off his mouth, wet his dry lips with his mostly dry tongue, and eased forward. In his mind's eye he could see back to when he was a shy 12 year old boy all over again, tryin' to dig up enough courage to kiss Matilda Millhouse. He remembered that first kiss an' wondered what all the fuss was about. Then he realized somethin'. That griz's breath was a lot like Matilda's had been. I guess jerky smells the same no matter who eats it. He broke out into a sweat. He'd never had to do anything this hard before.

He stretched out his neck an' puckered up his lips an' was jes' about to plant one on when a stick he hadn't seen—it WAS kinda dark—poked him in the ear. It took all he had to keep from bellerin' out. Kinda ruined the moment, you might say. After he dug the dirt outa his ear an' wiped the blood off....blood? BLOOD!! Here he was going to be just a few inches away from the top carnivore on earth and he was chummin' it along with his own fresh blood! He had to get this deed done quick if he planned on livin' much longer! He held his hand over the side of his head to protect it from more sticks an' gave that griz a quick peck on the side of the nose.

He backed up as much as he could an' waited. He didn't feel sleepy. No more tired than he'd been a little while ago. How long does it take? Was that ole Ute tellin' the truth?

After what seemed an eternity, he still wasn't tired or sleepy…jus' really nervous and scared. More scared than he'd ever been or thought he could be. Well, at least the griz was still asleep. That helped. He got to thinkin' maybe he should try again. This time with a little more gusto.

So, he squirmed up to that sleeping bag of death an' puckered up again. This time he planted an "honest to Charlotte, I got ya," kinda smooch right on the wet part of the nose. Then he scooted back to wait again. Nothin happened. If he ever lived through this somehow an' found that ole Ute, that ole gray scalp would come under new ownership!

He had no idea how long he'd been in that grizzly tomb, but it really didn't matter 'cause he couldn't get out anyway. He decided to try to get a little more comfortable an' think about it. Maybe he could come up with a plan. Finally, somehow he drifted off to sleep…

When he woke up, it was still kinda dark, but gettin' lighter. Storm musta broke an' daylight's comin. Somethin' didn't feel right an' he was all kinds of hungry. He was always hungry, but this was different. He was HUNGRY!

The griz was still a sleepin' but it'd stir a little every now an' then. He had to get outa there an' quick! Suddenly, the griz snorted a little an' opened its beady little eyes, blinked a couple times an' rolled over onto its other side. It was time to go! Ol' Frank was pretty groggy too an' his arms an' legs didn't feel right. He eased around an' got tangled up in his buckskins. Funny, they were kinda snug jus' a little while ago, now they seemed way too big. Must be another of those weird dreams he got after drinkin' too much. His right leg was asleep an' he started to rub some feelin' back into it. About the time the needles in his leg really woke up, so did the griz! Now it was really time to go!

He rolled over an' scrambled for the openin'. It seemed lots bigger than it was a little while ago. When he heard the griz pop its jaws once he got a shot of enthusiasm! He shot outa that den like a drunken sailor out of the pub at 4 am. His leg was still purty sleepy an' he was kinda wobbly, too.

Then he realized that most of the snow was gone! He also realized that he wasn't nearly as fat as he was the last time he'd checked. He was only half the man he used to be! He'd lost so much weight that his buckskins were trippin' him up. He wouldn't need 'em iff'n he was dead anyway, so he shucked 'em off in the griz's face an' tried to run. The griz was jus' as groggy an' wobbly as he was an' when he got those buckskins wrapped around his head, he kinda got lost an' it took a while for him to figure out what happened an' get 'em off.

Frank needed every second he could buy right now an' his account was runnin' purty low. He did the best he could to take advantage of the situation by taking a crash course in downhill skiin'. He still had his moccasins on his feet an' was doin' purty well for the first time. He didn't know how to turn, an' stoppin' wasn't an option, so down he went.

Meanwhile the griz had gotten undressed an' was comin' hard. Poor ol' Frank was runnin' outa luck an it looked like he was runnin' outa life here purty quick, too. Lookin' like the end was near. The griz was a gainin' on him an' the ski slope was a gettin' shorter.

Frank knew that the fastest way to go from point A to point B was a straight line an' he was a goin' as straight an' fast as he could. He jus' didn't know where point B was an' it was somewhat worrisome to think that point B was a catchin' up with him!

Well, like I said, the ski slope really was gettin' shorter, an' at the end of it was a big ol' cliff about a thousand feet down. Maybe only a couple hunnert, but the result was gonna be the same either which way. The thought of gettin' skewered by a tree or smeared all over the rocks below was some'at disconcertin' to him too. After givin' it some quick an' thorough contemplatin', he decided that iff'n he was goin' to be griz food, the griz was a goin' to have to go find him.

Frank flew off'n that cliff doin' 90 to nothin' an never looked back. He was mighty interested in his future right now an' scared that his past was a goin' to catch up to him any time now. The next thought he had was that if he spread his arms an' legs he wouldn't drop as fast an' would have more time to contemplate what limited future he had left.

Well, when he did that, an amazin' thing happened. All those months of hibernatin' had burnt off all his fat an' when he spread out his arms an' legs, all that loose skin gave him the same characteristics of a flyin' squirrel! (*Without the tail, of course.*)

After he stopped screamin'—I mean bellerin'—he found out that he was goin' to live longer than he'd thought an' started to enjoy the ride. That is, until he got cooled off from his ski run. Then he got cold. He was still purty high up on the mountain when he started his flight lesson an' then he caught an updraft an' went even higher! It actually helped him out by stiffenin' him up some. Then he got caught up in a hail storm that left little purple dots all over his back from gettin' whacked by all those hailstones makin' him one interestin' lookin' critter.

Well, he was headed away from the mountain an' could see the foothills down below with a hint of green grass a showin'. He began a gradual descent to the lower country when he spotted the tipi's. He headed towards 'em hopin' that after all he'd been through that day that they wouldn't kill him an' maybe they'd give 'im somethin' to eat. That's where he jus' kinda dropped in on us like I was sayin' earlier.

All the screachin' we heard was him a bellerin' when some of the arrows came a little too close for his comfort. Scared him. He won't admit it, but it did.

So, that's how Frank came to be known as the Bear Man… or the Bare Man. Your choice!

That's the honest truth or my name's not Rumplestiltskin!

CHAPTER 15

The Annual White River Ropin'

Welcome to the 12th annual White River Ropin'. Every Labor Day, ropers come from all over the country to attend and participate in this annual event. They come from Pee Ants Crick to Trappers Lake, from the Red Desert country in Wyoming to Colorado's Grand Valley in addition to a bunch from Utah's Uintah Basin and, of course, the local ropers on the lower White River. This is a big event for this region. Some of the most skilled twine throwers in the world look forward to it. Let me tell you, there is some mighty tough competition that shows up. But it's not just for ropers. There's cuttin' and team pennin' too. You'd best be payin' attention, a feller can go from first to last in an instant.

Now this isn't your run-of-the-mill rodeo. No sir! This is a one of a kind, never copied prairie dog ropin'/rodeo! Yup, I said prairie dogs! Never heard of it before? Well, you're about to.

How do we get our p-dogs you might ask? We have a couple p-dog towns we like to use that are reasonably flat and easy to get to. We alternate every year so we don't stress them out too much. Next, we erect a four foot high solid fence with gathering wings to funnel 'em into the arena. Then, we plug off about half the holes between the wings and drop smoke bombs down the others. Soon there are hundreds of p-dogs comin' out of the unplugged holes. Think lemmings! While they're coughin' and rubbin' their eyes, they're a little disoriented and fairly easy to drive into the pen. Of course, for some, this isn't their first rodeo so they're breakin' back tryin' to get away. This is the cuttin' part of the rodeo. These cowboys and cowgirls are ridin' low profile, super quick horses that can move so smooth and quick that they can literally cut a p-dog off it's hole!

Each competitor starts with 10 points and gets another five points for each p-dog they bring into the arena. They lose two points for each confirmed getaway. It gets pretty excitin' at this point 'cause the p-dogs are a goin' every which way with absolutely no regard for manners or protocol. It's almost impossible to stick with a single p-dog 'cause they duck, dodge and double back on you so much. They run under other riders' horses and sometimes grab and hold onto their tails. Heck, one even jumped onto a horse's head, ran up its neck and chased the cowboy out of the saddle! Then it commenced to chase the unseated rider all around town with his own horse! Some charitable soul finally roped the hostile little varmint out of the saddle and saved a very embarrassed cowboy from bein' run down by his own horse!

Well, after the dust had settled and the tally added up, Pee Ants Pete won the event with 22 points. He penned three, lost two and got a sportsmanship point for ropin' the recalcitrant rodent off the saddle. Comin' in second was Dixie from Savery Valley. She penned two and got credit for another when it was discovered that there was a p-dog hiding in her horse's tail. She lost two, which brought her score up to 21.

Some of the others had a tougher time. Latigo, the guy whose horse was commandeered by the p-dog, was obviously out of the money. Brewster Baggs had the misfortune of mistakin' a small badger for a p-dog in all the dust and excitement. That didn't go too well. His horse ducked back so quick that poor ole Brewster fell off right on top of the badger! That was bad enough, but one of the badgers back feet got caught in Brewster's belt. By the time they got pulled apart, his chaps looked like something the Kardashians would want to wear! He should be out of the hospital in a couple days.

The next event is the team ropin'. Since p-dogs hibernate some of the year, these ropers have to practice on whatever low profile critter they can find. Cats seem to be the most abundant and available. They're pretty interestin'. You can take a cat that is really laid back and docile, but when you put a rope on it, it gets all kinds of excited! Now it has a chance to do all the neat tricks and moves that just a minute ago, it hadn't even thought of! They have so much fun! Double backflips, triple gainers, pirouettes, they do 'em all! Sometimes they'll even let you know when they're done! They'll just lay down and watch you. Now, here's the tricky part. They want you to think they're done, but when you go to take the rope off, they start doing their tricks all over again! I think that while they were laying there that they were thinking of new tricks to do! All good things must come to an end so now you have to turn the cat loose. They can get pretty grouchy about it. They may even try to bite or scratch you because they were having such a good time and really don't want it to end. Alas, there are other cats to entertain, so you turn it loose.

Now back to the team ropin'. P-dogs aren't that fast, but they're pretty quick. So when they're turned loose out of the chute *(that happens to be a short 4" diameter pipe)*, you don't have to break the barrier for good time. The time starts when the p-dog crosses the barrier line. With the p-dogs bein' so small, the header often becomes the heeler when they don't jerk their slack quick enough and the p-dog runs through the loop. Most of the time that ends up bein' called a "double hocker" even though p-dogs don't have hocks. In other words both hind feet get caught. Body catches don't count. Sometimes only one back foot gets caught and there's no penalty for that, but if you catch both hind feet you get one second knocked off your time. Same with a head catch since they're so small. If you end up with a front leg in the loop with the head there's no penalty, just no bonus time.

Each team gets three loops, so if you miss twice you're out of the money. Lots of teams will gamble and throw at the same time, hoping to catch both ends at the same time. Sometimes it works and it's fun when it does, but this is where left handed ropers are in high demand if they're any good.

These are specialized ropes too. They're small diameter nylon reinforced with steel wire for body and tooth resistance. They range from fairly stiff to almost floppy. It all depends on personal preference. Also, they're only 15 feet long. That makes it so you actually have to chase the p-dog instead of throwin' from long distance.

The "arena" is a relatively flat place with all but two of the holes filled in and packed tight. Since these p-dogs live here, they know where every hole is and that's where they'll go…just as fast as they can. At the far end is where these holes are located. From the chute to the holes is only about 120 feet so the ropers have to be pretty quick on the draw. This is where all the off season cat ropin' practice comes in to play. Cats are lots faster than P-dogs so those who practiced have a definite advantage over those who didn't, and it shows.

First up was a brother/sister team from the Uintah Basin country, Cory and Tory McNeely. They placed third last year but would've won except the p-dog kicked a foot out of the heel loop before the judge dropped the time flag. Now if the rumors are even close to bein' right, there isn't a cat in the whole Uintah Basin that doesn't have rope burns on it somewhere. These two are hungry for a championship.

It's the luck of the draw on which p-dog you get. The one closest to the chute is the next one up. The McNeely's drew a young of the year p-dog. That just means this years pup. They generally run faster than the older fat adults. Sounds familiar, doesn't it? It shot out of that chute like a bullet out of a gun barrel but Cory was able to catch the head and a front leg about 50 feet from the chute. Tory flipped her loop out and caught both hind feet before it got to do any fancy dancin'. Pretty impressive!

Next up were Jed and Ramon from Powder Wash country up north. They ran into some bad luck last year when Jed's horse Speedball, got the rope wrapped around his legs and got chewed up by a highly agitated p-dog. Speedball appeared to be pretty well healed up, although he seemed like he was tryin' to stomp on any p-dog that came close to him! It took Jed a little longer to catch his, but he caught the head alone and Ramon gathered up both back feet in a hurry. With the bonus second, they beat the McNeely's time by a tenth of a second.

Just watchin' these guys catch these p-dogs is amazin'. These are highly skilled ropers, but one of the other things that draws people from all over the country is the wrecks. Animals and wrecks just seem to go together, and this get-together was no different.

You can tell the ropers that haven't had any cats to practice on. Especially those who are used to ropin' calves. Rowdy and Marlin are prime examples. Rowdy threw his rope and caught his p-dog right behind the shoulders. At that point he realized that it was too late for a head catch and too early for the feet so he threw it a little slack and as the rope slid back, he jerked it tight again. The problem was, he forgot to adjust his adrenalin level from calves to p-dogs. P-dogs only weigh a couple pounds so when he jerked his slack, that p-dog came flyin' back to Marlin. The rope wrapped around his neck with the p-dog securely caught in the mess! Well, Rowdy got his horse shut down but for some reason Marlin forgot to stop his right away. Rowdy still had a pretty good hold on his rope and realized-a little late- that it was getting' pretty snug before he turned it loose!

Meanwhile Marlin had gotten all tangled up in his own rope and was gettin' all snuggly with Ms. P-dog. Somehow his rope had flanked up his horse and the horse was showin' his disapproval of the arrangement by tryin' to get rid of these unwanted hitch hikers that were doin' a great job of sackin' him out every time he jumped! Marlin would've gladly gotten off, but he was so tangled up in the ropes that he couldn't! To make matters worse, the p-dog wasn't that fond of horseback ridin' either! She was chewin' on whatever she could sink her teeth into. Think sewin' machine without the thread.

It was pretty excitin' there for a while. The rodeo fans were hollerin' for Marlin, his horse, the p-dog, or just hollerin' 'cause that's what you do at rodeos. The PETA protesters were hollerin' for the p-dog to go for Marlin's jugular…peacefully, of course. When all was said and done, Marlin had a few extra holes in his shirt and eventually ended up with several vaccinations after leaving the EMT tent. His horse finally calmed down and ended up with a few rope burns for his trouble. The p-dog was a different story. She appeared to be havin' a rough go of it. There she was, layin' out there in the arena flat on her back…apparently lifeless when suddenly, here comes the PETA paramedics team!

They leaped over the arena wall and rushed to the side of their fallen hero…except the chubby one, he tripped and fell several times and by the time he finally made it to the fallen victim, he needed medical attention too. The PETA paramedics immediately began CPR on the rodent while the EMT's worked on the chubby guy. The head PETA guy started chest compressions not realizin' that the reason they were workin' on the little bugger was because of the compressions she'd just received while on the horse!

All was quiet in the stands and arena as we all watched the PETA patrol and EMT's at work. As the PETA paramedic finished the chest compressions, he put his ear close to the p-dog's mouth to listen for any breathin'. Not hearin' or feelin' any, he proceeded to give it mouth to mouth rescue breathin'. The next thing we knew, he jumped up and started doin' the Cheyenne war cry accompanied by a Hopi rain dance! Who knew that this goofy guy was bilingual! Only then did we see that the p-dog was fastened securely to his bottom lip! Now he had an idea of what Marlin had just gone through! For some reason he didn't appear to appreciate the snuggles and loves Ms. P-dog was givin' him. After he and she performed a magnificent display of dancing and chanting, Ms. p-dog had had enough and ended the relationship leaving her partner a little worse for wear and with a hole in his lip to remember her by. Now it was his turn for shots!

This rodeo was gettin' more and more interestin' all the time! Well, Jed and Ramon ended up winnin' the team ropin' with the McNeelys right behind them. Not bad for their second try!

Team pennin's up next. Now this event can get kinda wild at times. A team consists of two riders and a gate man. The gate man can be mounted or on foot. Most are mounted. Too many instances of p-dogs runnin' up a guys leg under his chaps. Seems like after they get to a snug place, they start diggin' and it gets mighty uncomfortable!

Twenty p-dogs are turned loose in the arena at one time. Each group of four are colored the same so there's five groups. The teams have three minutes to gather as many of their color into the pen as they can while keepin' the other colors out.

Now, there has only been two times in the history of the rodeo that a team has accomplished this in the allotted time. Teams have tried a variety of different methods, from the classical herd cut to pushing as many as will fit into the pen and cutting out the ones you don't want. It's pretty similar to chasin' a particular fly into a particular room when there's a dozen of them flyin' around!

Each team starts at the ropin' chute and as they cross the line between the timers their time starts and a flag with the color of p-dogs they're supposed to gather up is dropped for all to see. The gate man hurries to the 6X6 foot square pen and opens the gate. The riders try to follow their preplanned strategy the best they can. About this time, the p-dogs are acting more like a bunch of mice that were hidin' under an overturned bale of hay. They scatter all over the place lookin' for a hole to hide in.

For a while there it looked like the team from Whitewater was gonna get 'em all, but Elwood the gate guy slammed the gate too early while makin' the final cut and squashed a wrong colored p-dog just as time ran out.

Here comes the PETA paramedics again! This time the chubby guy and Squirt (*the guy with the newly and naturally pierced lip*) didn't come. It was pretty evident to most that this was this p-dog's last rodeo. The PETA's didn't bother to do the CPR thing this time. They brought a stethoscope! It didn't appear as though any wanted to try to resuscitate the poor thing, either. Maybe Squirt was the only one who knew how and he was going to need a plug in his lip before any more attempts!

Well, after determinin' that the patient was deceased, they pulled out a little black body bag and gently placed the corpse inside and solemnly left the arena proclaimin' their intent to file murder charges against Elwood and everyone else affiliated with the rodeo. They got indignant all over again when Chu Lin offered to give it a proper burial.

It had long been suspected that Chu Lin's "rat on a stick" came from a p-dog town! He ran a mobile catering service he called the PETA Pantry. A fun acronym for People Eating Tasty Animals. We all called it the Roach Coach. Maybe the PETA paramedics didn't see the humor in it. People like that never do.

Even with the dark pall of death permeatin' the atmosphere, the competitors somehow pressed on, although Chu Lin's business slowed down quite a bit! As it turned out, the Whitewater team ended up winnin' the event with the teams from Marvine ranch and South Fork tyin' for second. They don't have access to cats like most did. They practice on "picket pins". They're small squirrels that dig holes all over their pastures and they're mighty quick. A lot like small p-dogs.

The final event was the tie down ropin'. The earlier events are pretty excitin'…especially with the clowns…er the PETA folks…but the tie down ropin' is the one event that brings in the most people and interest. It's just like calf ropin' 'cept on a smaller scale. This is where the steel strands in the rope as well as steel mesh gloves come in handy. Instead of ropers just usin' one glove like for team ropin', they wear gloves on both hands for obvious reasons. Now, everybody has their own ideas on how to go about throwin' and tyin' p-dogs. They all follow the rope to the p-dog, but here's where things differ a little. Some pick up the rope with the p-dog danglin' by the neck and slip the tie string around a front leg, then they step on the rope and pull the tie string snug so they don't get bit and try to wrap up the hind feet that're goin' as fast as they can move. Others will grab the hind legs and stretch 'em out, then loop a front leg and wrap up the hind feet. It takes someone who is quick and coordinated to git 'er done! Either way can work if you practice enough.

The p-dogs have to stay tied for five seconds after "time" is called. You don't have to worry about untyin' 'em. After about ten seconds they'll chew their way out. Tie strings aren't reusable. Oh, and another thing, p-dogs have to be on the ground when you go to "throw" and tie 'em. If you happen to jerk your slack too hard (*it happens in the heat of competition*) and the p-dog lands in the saddle with you, you have to set it on the ground before tyin' it up. It's a safety issue. Too many ropers and horses have gotten chewed up by takin' the shortcut. Not to mention the damage done to the saddle and tack.

So, our first tie down roper comes from Rifle, Colorado. He attended last year as a spectator and decided he wanted to compete this trip. I don't recall his real name, we ended up callin' him Winch, which is short for

Winchester. He was ridin' a bay horse he called Bullet. Interestin', Rifle, Winchester and Bullet! This horse was aptly named 'cause when that p-dog came out of the chute, he came out of the box like a shot! Winch made a great throw and caught that p-dog right away. Problem was bullets don't stop until they either hit somethin' or run out of power. Well, Bullet didn't stop and he hardly noticed the little two pound drag that was a p-dog flyin' behind him. Neither was he intimidated by the four foot high fence that he was rapidly approachin'. He easily cleared the fence and kept goin' with the p-dog sailin' along behind.

The PETA patrol came a runnin' and screamin', but Bullet kept on a goin' with no regard for their shriekin' and orders to halt! Poor Winch! He made a great catch but still got a "no time" for leavin' the arena. We may never know the fate of the flyin' p-dog! Chu Lin was watchin' pretty closely through his binoculars, though!

Next up was a local favorite, Clancy. Clancy was raised in a p-dog town and had a pretty good idea what they'd do in most any situation. He was ridin' a short dun horse he called Tracker. Everyone likes a winner and this team was tough to beat. Tracker had also been raised around p-dog holes, so to say that he was sure footed was a gross understatement. He could glide through most p-dog towns at top speed without ever seemin' to look down. He was also pretty well trained. When Clancy threw his rope, Tracker was droppin' his hocks in the dirt. Clancy never had to jerk his slack, just step off and head down the rope. Sometimes this caused a little bit of a problem. If the rope jerked tight when the p-dog had all four feet off the ground, they'd fly up in the air. Sometimes right back to Clancy. One time when this happened, he tried to catch it with his hands and it ended up inside his shirt! Let me tell you, brother, Michael Jackson never dreamed of doin' some of the moves Clancy made that day!

Today, though, he had his shirt all buttoned up and he was all business. He even took the stampede string off his hat to make sure there was one less thing that could go wrong. He and Tracker made a clean break out of the box and caught that p-dog in nothin' flat. When Clancy picked up the p-dog to tie it down, he saw that instead of catching it around the neck, the rope was in its mouth and around the back of its head. Still a legal catch, just a little more difficult to deal with as the P-dog was about to pull it off its head! Quick thinkin' and actin' saved the day and as he pulled the p-dog tight the rope caught in its teeth and Clancy was able to get the deed done with no damage done to anyone in 8.6 seconds!

Cory McNeely was up next. He and his horse got a clean break out of the box and caught the p-dog almost as fast as Clancy. As he bailed off his horse, his spur caught the cantle on his saddle and tripped him up. He got up and in two jumps was tyin' the p-dog up. His time was 10.2 seconds.

Jax from Rock Springs was next. He won the event last year and planned on repeatin' the task. Now Jax was different. Not just the way he acted, everything he did was different. I kinda think he did it on purpose. He rode an Aussie saddle on a burro. Yup, a burro. I told you he was different! The burro's name was Cactus and his disposition was just as prickly as his name! Obviously Cactus wasn't as fast as the horses that he was goin' up against. He didn't have to be. He and Jax had a technique that was nearly unbeatable. Cactus would put his chest up against the barrier and when the p-dog came out of the chute he only had to run 15 or 20 feet before Jax threw his rope. Jax seldom, if ever, missed.

Well, here it was crunch time again. Things were goin' perfectly until the PETA Chihuahua mysteriously found its way into the arena at the same time the p-dog was released. Now, Cactus was almost fool proof, but, like I said, he had a somewhat prickly disposition. He didn't like unfamiliar people—especially women—horses, cattle, sheep, or even p-dogs. I don't even think he liked Jax, except after a ropin' run he'd always give Cactus a carrot. Cactus liked carrots. But he hated dogs with a passion. Especially noisy, yappin' little doglets like this one that was comin' his way. Somethin' in the primeval past, I guess.

When that noisy disturber of the peace came yappin' at the p-dog, Cactus took off after it. The p-dog saw all the excitement and decided to go back to the chute and hide. Meanwhile, Jax is tryin' unsuccessfully to get a handle on Cactus and Cactus is chasin' that doglet all around the arena tryin to bite or stomp it to death.

As the PETA folks watched, they realized with horror that they were about to sacrifice their mascot to an angry burro so they set out on a rescue mission to the arena! Big mistake! By now, Cactus had the doglet by the tail and was doin' his best to shorten the tail with his teeth by shakin' it like a rag doll! About the time the doglet and its tail parted ways, two of the PETA folks were right there screamin' mean things to one or both of the contestants.

To say that Jax and Cactus were in a somewhat agitated state would be puttin' it mildly. Cactus clamped onto the shoulder of the chubby guy and started doin' the rag doll shake again. Jax roped the other one and had her thrown down and tied up before she could say, "Save the whales!"

This mobilized the rest of the PETA patrol. When they charged into the arena intent on saving their comrades, they failed to notice several ropers waitin' at the gates! Oh what fun these ropers had! It didn't take long before all the PETA patrol was securely thrown and tied. Three were headed and heeled and the rest were just roped and tied.

Someone was pokin' around in the PETA paramedics trailer and found some vaccine and syringes. After considerin' the welfare of these unfortunate folks, it was decided that they probably really needed vaccinated against all the terrible diseases that they could be exposed to while out saving the animals. Now these folks were makin' a lot of noise already, but when the cowboys came at 'em with those needles, they cranked up the volume so that every coyote within 20 miles started to howl! Needless to say, they all got shots for everythin' from Parvo to Bubonic Plague. They should be safe for quite a while!

The sheriff and deputies showed up about that time. After checkin' to make sure the tie ropes had regulation knots to prevent disqualification, they untied all of 'em and gave them a free ride to jail and charged them all with disturbin' the peace and bein' public nuisances!

Throughout all this, the spectators were goin' wild with applause! Most said that it was the best rodeo ever, and to make sure to invite the PETA folks again next year. Chu Lin would make it a point to have plenty of his now famous "rats on a stick" in his PETA Pantry truck!

CHAPTER 16

Vegans vs Real People

The Plight of Plants

I've heard it said that Vegans are real people and I'll have to agree that some are pretty good folks…at least the ones I know seem to be. However, there are those who make me wonder. They're the ones I'm writing about.

You know, the type that feels that if you don't agree with them that you're a blight on planet Earth and maybe even the Moon. Those who feel it a terrible wrong that anyone would even consider deriving any usefulness from any animal in any form. Some even shun those who enjoy a bit of cheese every now and then. Cheese comes from milk and milk happens to come from lactating mammals that have hooves. Other mammals produce milk and everybody knows that dogs are a man's best friend, but that friendship only goes so far. Just once, I'd like to see someone hook a cat up to a milking machine and turn it on! You'd probably get the same result trying to hold a cat while running a dust buster! Yet "the purists" look down their long, self righteous noses at anyone who would even consider such a vile act. They consider it exploiting the natural way life should be.

"The Purists" are the point of this thing. First of all, let me make myself clear. There are some plants that are good to eat. Especially their derivatives like sugar and chocolate. I really like bread, too. For now, though, I'll concentrate on vegetables because I've grown and eaten a few in my lifetime—sometimes under duress, but I've eaten them just the same.

A major complaint from these people about my lifestyle is that I eat meat. I like meat. It tastes good and is a great source of natural protein. They claim that red meat is bad for you so I cook mine until it's brown. Some plants are high in protein too, but they don't taste as good as meat. Granted, not all meat is equal. Some tastes better than others. Terrestrial meat is much better than any meat grown in water.

Most of what I eat was owned by the government. I have to buy a license hoping to be able to find the critter so I can kill it (*I know the politically correct phrase these days is "harvest" so be offended if you want to. It's your choice.*) Then, I take it home, process it, and store it until it's time to eat it. Herein lies the major rift that really keeps these people up at night- the killing part. "How can you look into those beautiful, innocent brown eyes and want to kill it," they say. Just ask any homeowner who just had $5000 worth of trees and shrubs stripped bare from an antler bearing ungulate that question! Besides, I don't look at their eyes. I'm looking at the future food storage my family will need to live on for the next year. Yes, I agree that they are beautiful animals, but they're also food.

That leads into the next part. Don't most gardeners take pride in their produce? They plant, water, nurture and harvest. Same as a rancher. We plant cows in an area that will feed them and keep them healthy. We turn the bulls into them to be fertilized for the next crop. In the fall, we wean the calves and sell them. That's our harvest cycle. Wild game is similar, except we don't have any control over the genetics, that's nature's job. However, we do take part in range management and the "harvest" of surplus animals.

"But you KILL the animals!" you say. Yes, we do. Did you ever try to eat a LIVING deer or elk? Tough to do! It's a lot more humane than what you do to your garden plants. Let me explain:

Generally, from the time the trigger is pulled until the animal is completely dead, only a few seconds go by. Whereas your plants are tortured sometimes for months on end before they're killed and dead. At least animals have a means of escape! Your plants are rooted in fear. They can't get away!

"Preposterous!" you say, but is it? Plants have to be alive to grow just like animals. You are not as innocent as you thought all this time. You are also, directly or indirectly, an agent of death! It's one of the laws of nature: something has to die in order for something else to live. That's just the way it is.

You may say it's not the same, but isn't it? Just because it doesn't try to get away (*because it can't*) is it okay to kill it? "It doesn't have any feelings!" How do you know? Just because you can't hear them scream or cry out, does that make you feel better and justify your superior moral position?

Let's talk about some examples of the victims that suffer in silence. Why do you think they're called 'heads' of lettuce? First of all, you decapitate them from their only source of nourishment, effectively ending any future it might have had. Then you take them into your home—a place supposedly of peace and safety—unless you happen to be a vegetable! When it's time to make a salad, you rip and shred the innocent head until it's reduced to a pile of slowly dying shredded leaves.

Next comes the beautiful tomatoes you've bragged to your neighbors about. They're a little more dramatic as their life blood—you call it juice and seeds—flows out all over the execution board. Carrots are next. Yeah, the ones that were living underground hiding and doing their best to stay out of the way; they weren't causing anyone any trouble. First, you rip them out of their warm, comfortable home, then you wash them off and then, with a primeval almost savage glee, you proceed to skin them alive. Yes, I said it: they're still living! As if that wasn't enough, you then hack and slice until they fit your idea of what they should be according to your unconscionable plan for the day.

Now, speaking of skinning alive, what about onions? At least they have a small defense mechanism. Think about it the next time they make you cry. Their cries are unheard, unheralded and uncared for.

The poor cabbage! They are probably treated with the least respect and most disgrace of them all. After you cut, shred, hack and whack these poor defenseless heads into small strips of what used to be a proud, beautiful specimen, they are left to rot in their own juices (cabbage blood) until they are spoiled enough to become sauerkraut. The indignity is almost more than any person with even a hint of a conscience can bear!

What about potatoes? They're also extirpated from their warm, comfortable, supposedly safe home in the ground only to suffer the ignominious fate of having their eyes plucked out while other family members watch and shudder, knowing that they are going to be next. What's the matter? Can't stand to have something that's still alive watch as you sadistically desecrate the body of a lowly tuber? Just try to look the next potato in the eyes before you torture, slaughter and eat it and tell yourself that you're not a heartless sadist deep down. Think of how the Tuber family must feel as they watch in horror while you repeatedly stab one of their own innocents with a fork before baking it alive! Or when you slice or shred the body only to drop into boiling oil! At least that death is relatively quick after their torture.

Peas are pulled from the mother plant's womb, ripped open with horrific glee to expose the small, innocent spheres of life. Tell me, where's the compassion?

Corn is stripped naked of its husks for the whole world to see, only to be boiled or broiled for a treat. Have you no shame? No mercy? Where's the decency in life?

Let us talk of the lingering slow deaths of peppers and others as they are left to die when their life blood slowly dries up and they become dried, wrinkled shells of their former glory and their carcasses hung up for decoration, trophies, if you will. Gruesome, just gruesome. I could go on but I am sick at heart from addressing all this malicious butchery, gore and heinous savagery.

If you don't grow a garden but buy your produce from a store, are you any less culpable? You pay mercenaries to do the dirty work for you. The vegetables are already processed and frozen in a bag or cooked to death in a can. Perhaps you pick out your fresh vegetables from the store cooler? That is just a morgue for plants.

Even Jesus, after his resurrection asked for meat. He didn't ask for a Jerusalem artichoke or an Armenian cucumber. He's a heavenly being and wanted heavenly food! He wanted MEAT! All they had was a broiled fish, so he chased it down with some honey.

The old saying "you are what you eat" holds true here. Would you like to be compared to a beautiful deer or elk, or is the image that comes to mind a lumpy squash, a bug eyed potato or maybe a skinny pole bean?

"But we help the environment with renewable resources," you say. Wait a minute, don't you think animals are renewable? The plants convert greenhouse gasses into oxygen and your efforts cause the premature deaths of untold billions of innocent plants. It stops every good thing they could have done! On the other hand, if I kill an elk, that saves about 10 pounds of oxygen producing plants every day! That is three thousand six hundred fifty pounds per year! For a five year old elk, that comes to 9 ¼ TONS for its lifetime! Where is the greater benefit?

Now, don't get me wrong. I enjoy a great baked potato with sour cream and butter with my steak as much as anyone and maybe even some mixed vegetables (as long as they don't come out of a can). I'm just trying to point out the hypocrisy that we have to deal with every day while putting up with, or listening to, your narrow minded, self righteous rhetoric! I just wanted you to know the other side of the story. Not that you really care.

By the way, my food is never tortured and is dead long before it's cooked!

CHAPTER 17

Bonny

She walked steadily down the hallway trying not to be noticed. She was a little taller and bigger boned than the average high school girl. Her gaze was downcast, her shoulders slumped so much that she nearly appeared to be hunchbacked at times. Stringy dark hair shrouded her face. She wasn't pretty. All these things contributed to her low self-esteem, that is, if she had any at all.

This was during the time when, if you didn't get good enough grades, you were held back another year. This had happened to her more than once. Her brother joined us a few years earlier and wasn't having as rough a time as she was, although it wasn't easy for him either.

As far as I could tell, she had no friends; and that's a bad place to be when you are surrounded by teenagers whose whole world revolves around being popular. If you are popular, you have a lot of friends—even if you don't happen to like them! It's kind of like politics 101!

One of our classmates happened to be a boy who was quite possibly the most obnoxious person that I have ever known. (*Please don't take this as a challenge! If there are any worse, I don't want to meet them!*) Anyway, he would go out of his way to ridicule and make fun of her. He seemed to relish flattening himself against the opposite wall in the hallway, feigning absolute terror and loudly warning everyone to watch out as she walked by. A few people would laugh at him for being so ridiculous and walk on by, but, because it got him the attention he wanted, it became an every time thing. Her brother even decided to get in on the act a few times for the attention. She would just drop her head a little lower and keep walking, not looking right or left, just at the floor in front of her feet.

Her name was Bonny. When she talked, which wasn't very often, it was a low mumble, scarcely discernible. In all the years we were in school, I don't think I ever saw her smile, that is, until our senior year. She was one of the "Invisible People". Unpopular. Seldom seen. Never heard. A loner. Someone who didn't exist, as far as some people were concerned.

During our senior year, something wonderful happened. Another girl in similar circumstances moved in. She and Bonny became good friends. They would walk down the hallway, side by side talking away as good friends do. I was happy for her, but still kept my distance. I didn't tease her as some still did; I just did my thing and let her do hers.

After we graduated, we all scattered, as kids that age tend to do. A few years later, I was surprised to hear that she'd gotten married. She was a mail-order bride before social media went to the Dot Com era.

She and her husband ran a filling station in the middle of the Chevron oil field. On occasion, I would need to stop in for a filter or something. The first time I went, she was behind the counter and greeted me in a calm, confident voice. I had to look again to make sure she was the same Bonny I'd gone to school with a few years earlier. She was the same person physically to a point, but that was all. She had found her self worth and with that came self-confidence. Working in the station forced her to get out of her comfort zone (*more of a shell*) and look people in the eyes and talk with them. No longer did she carry her head down and her shoulders slumped. No longer did she mumble when she spoke. She spoke clearly and confidently. Again, I was happy for her.

A few more years went by and I happened to see her in one of the restaurants in town. There she was, sitting at a table, her shiny, bald head out there for everyone to see. No pretentiousness, no shame. She didn't seem the least bit embarrassed with her appearance. She had been through much worse in school. Again, she greeted me in the same calm, matter-of-fact way as before. The chemotherapy had taken her hair but neither it nor the cancer would ever diminish her self worth.

If she ever blamed me personally for what had to have been the toughest years of her life in school, she never gave any indication of it. She seemed at peace with life, holding, it appeared, no animosity or bitterness toward others. Not long after I last saw and actually visited with her, the cancer claimed her as another victim. The cancer killed her body but couldn't touch her spirit. What a great example of forgiveness!

Thank you, Bonny.

CHAPTER 18

The Goose Hunt

"No goose today?" It was more of a statement than a question from my dad.

"I can't get close to the geese. They're too far away. That's the problem with living out here. The wheat fields are a mile across and the geese stay in the middle where you can't get close enough to shoot. I'm going to get my rifle. They're so thick, I'll just aim in the middle of the flock and pull the trigger. I should get at least one, maybe two or three!"

"You're not supposed to use a rifle, it's illegal."

"If that's the case, I'll never get a goose. I haven't had one in two or three years!"

"How come Jason gets geese with his shotgun? He seems to bring them in pretty regular."

"I don't know, he's pretty smug about it. He says that I just need to learn how to hunt. I sure would like to plug his barrel! He's the only one around here that gets any geese and no one I know of has given him permission to hunt their place."

"We've got to move the yearlings from the south pasture to the canyon pasture today. Might as well get your horse caught and saddled."

The south pasture was planted with winter wheat and was coming along pretty well. There were some geese there but not in the numbers of other places. The canyon pasture had running water and pretty good grass. The cattle moved along pretty well. They were used to being handled. What bothered me was the way the geese acted while I was moving the cattle. They didn't seem the least bit bothered and I think that if I'd had my shotgun, I could have picked one off!

That got me to thinkin'. Now that the cattle would be gone, the geese would be suspicious of me just riding through. I'd heard of guys making a sort of blind by cutting out the shape of a cow from a piece of plywood, then hiding behind it while moving in close enough for a shot. I thought it might be worth a try so I started looking around for my "cow".

We didn't have any plywood, but I thought I could use some cardboard from the box our new water heater came in. Not as big as I'd like, but it was all I could find. Desperate times call for desperate measures, right? Well, it kind of looked like a cow. Hopefully, the geese wouldn't know any different or notice the size 9 leather boots on only two legs!

Right away, they could tell that this cow was a genetic defect with only two legs that walked sideways. It was something to stay away from, but with patience, I was able to work my way within range. The problem was I was carrying my shotgun in my left hand and had my right hand and arm stuck in the loops I had taped to the cardboard. I still needed to chamber a round too. Now what?!

I managed to move my gun to my right hand while it was still in the loop handhold and tried to quietly chamber a round. That was all these nervous geese needed. Cows didn't sound like that, didn't move like that, and didn't look like that! As they started to take off, I brought my gun up only to find that my cardboard cow kept me from seeing the rapidly departing geese. But, like the old saying goes,"When there's lead in the air, there's danger boys"!

Somehow, out of three shots, I got one! I'd shot half my cow away, but I got one! I was one proud hunter! I decided to drop by the filling station on my way home, even though it was way out of my way, to show off my prize. As I was telling the boys all about it, here comes Jason.

"Finally scared one to death, did ya? How long has it been dead before you found it and picked it up?" he chided as he lifted his limit of geese out of the back of his truck. "I'm going to have to grind a bunch of these up for jerky. I have so many in the freezer that I'm out of room!"

I didn't like that guy. Maybe this wasn't the best way to look at it, but somehow, some way, I needed to show him up. At least get a limit of geese one time!

Later, while riding through the pasture on my horse, it came to me. Possibly not the best idea, but seriously intriguing! I would hunt from the back of my horse! I know I'd thought of it earlier, but this wouldn't be a stealth attack. This would be a full on charge kind of like the Sioux on a buffalo hunt, only with geese! I would charge the flock from the saddle before they got away. Geese usually take a few steps before they get airborne and then it takes some distance before they're high enough to be out of range! Great idea! Fool proof! What could go wrong? Right?

When I told my dad about my brilliant scheme, his right eyebrow raised up like it always does when whatever is being discussed is either thought provoking or dangerous. In this instance, it may be both!

After going over the details like which horse to ride, how to make sure the horse didn't get shot or deafened by shooting next to his head, he gave me a tentative OK to go ahead with it. Then, he asked where all this was going to happen and if I was going alone or would someone go along with me. Where it would happen would depend on where the geese were at. As far as company went, I hadn't given that much thought. I had just assumed that I'd be the Lone Ranger, but after thinking about it I realized others might be interested in this Once-In-a-Lifetime experience. Dad recommended asking Bud if he'd be willing to let me hunt his place. So, over to Bud's I went.

"If there's ten out there, there's a thousand," he told me after giving me permission to hunt.

"How are ya gonna git a shot? They're all outta range for a shotgun."

I then explained my plan to him. As I did, his eyes brightened up, he sat up straight and said, "By jiminy, if I wasn't so stove up and had a horse, I'd go with ya!" Then he added, "That Jason has asked me a couple times if he could hunt out there and I've always told him no. Somethin' about him...He just seems kinda slimy to me. When are ya plannin' this attack?"

I told him I'd try first thing in the morning. He was fine with that and said he'd be watching from the knob on the north side of the field. Great!

Just as I was getting in my truck, Charlie, Bud's hired man, stopped me and asked if he could come along. He said he had his own horse and shotgun. But he was old—probably nearing 60. I was concerned that, at his "advanced age," it was a wise thing for him to even consider, but I told him that I'd meet him at the west end of the field at 6am. He said he'd be there.

When I got home, Mom told me that a couple of my friends had called and wanted me to call them back asap. It seemed my plan was being scattered around and they wanted in on the action. Henry was the first call I made. He was a serious contender for calf roping in the high school rodeo finals every year and a good friend of mine. I asked him if his horse had ever been shot around and if he thought this might mess with his horse's mind. He would ride a different horse than his calf roping horse and he'd be there on time.

Claude and I had been buddies since kindergarten. He and I were on the same level at a lot of things. Not really good or bad at anything. Just average and happy just to be there and contribute when possible.

Jerry hung around with Claude and I. We watched out for each other and tried to stay out of trouble. He was the smart one of the bunch. One of the classes he was taking was calculus. I think it has something to do with teeth.

Marcus. He is a little different. When he asked to join the hunt, he commented that he was a dedicated skeet shooter. In fact, he was so obsessed with it that his mom limited him to only a thousand rounds a week.

"Wow!" I said. "There must be a BUNCH of skeets around your place! Are they any good to eat?"

He chuckled as if I'd made a good joke and said that he went to the trap club to shoot them. (*I still don't know if they are good to eat; but he has a cute sister and I might need a date for homecoming, so he's coming*).

I had to turn the others down. Six would be plenty. I didn't need an army. I'd stick with a platoon, and I didn't want to impose on Bud. He was already being pretty generous. I hooked the horse trailer up to the truck, caught my horse and penned him up, then left my shotgun and shells in the truck so I wouldn't forget anything.

It took forever for 5am to show up. I hadn't slept much all night and wasn't at all sleepy or tired when I got out of bed. I went out and gave my horse a little hay and grain. Mom had the bacon and eggs waiting on the table for me with a big glass of udder cola (*that would be milk for city folks*). I slammed them down, thanked Mom, and headed outside. As I was getting in the truck after loading my horse, Dad stopped me, looked me in the eyes and told me to be careful and to watch out for others because they probably wouldn't.

Everyone was on time except for Jerry. He finally showed up just as it was getting to be good shooting light. He couldn't find his breast collar and that's why he was late. Since he came down a different road than the rest of us, he said he noticed a truck parked on the south side of the field in the brush. It looked like it might have been Jason's but he wasn't sure.

It didn't take long to saddle up. Everyone looked to be pretty well mounted except for Marcus. His horse was a fat, squatty little mare that looked to be built more for feed than speed. When asked if that's all he had to ride, he replied that he had a plan. She had really good speed for about 300 yards, then she would run out of gas which was why he brought her. OK. Why? He brought two shotguns, one for each hand. He wasn't worried about her running away because she was so fat. By the time the shooting got over, she'd be done too. I wasn't too sure that this was a good idea, but let's roll with it. He only needed an eye patch to look like Rooster Cogburn from the movie True Grit! His sister came along and wanted to video the whole thing for her

YouTube channel. She got quick interviews with each of us then headed over to the north knob to video us with Bud. I guess she had a big fancy lens on her camera that could bring us all up close and personal from that far away.

Our plan was to all line up about 20 yards apart in a skirmish line and walk our horses toward the geese that were still about 600 yards away. When they started to get nervous and acting like they were going to fly, we'd hook the spurs to ours horses and start shooting when we got close enough. Simple, right? Again, what could possibly go wrong with such a foolproof plan as this?

We mounted up with me on the right side and Charlie on the left flank. Charlie had three shells in his left hand with his reins and had his shotgun cradled in the crook of his right arm. Claude was next to him with Jerry on his right. Next was Marcus. He had a long roping rein draped across the swells of his saddle along with a shotgun in each hand. I hoped his horse didn't stumble! Henry was between us, reins in his left hand and, like Charlie, his shotgun cradled in the crook of his right arm.

This was it. Would this plan work? Would we survive intact? You never know until after it's all over. Here we were, men riding six abreast. In my mind I could hear the theme song for the movie "The Good, The Bad, and The Ugly". I even had the twitch on the right side of my face like Clint Eastwood would get just before the serious action started. da DAH da DA Daahh Wah WAAH Waahh….(*I guess you had to be there*)! Six desperate men with blood in their eyes and shells in their guns with one mission to accomplish….GET THE GEESE!

The horses could sense the excitement and were prancing along ready to be turned loose to run. It was reminiscent of the famous mile long cavalry charge the Australian Light Horsemen made in WW1 across the desert facing an entrenched enemy with rifles trained on them the whole way. As far as we knew, we weren't going to be shot at, but the comparison was fun to think about! No room for fear! No room for cowardice! Move on boldly against the odds! Forward and Onward!

When we were about 300 yards from the geese it seemed like every goose out there was watching us. Their heads were up, necks stretched as high as they could go, looking like a thousand submarine periscopes sticking out of the sea, only it was a sea of wheat stubble instead of water.

Another 50 yards and they started to get nervous. We held the line. 25 more yards and they were slowly waddling away. Another 25 yards and they started moving faster and sounding their alarm honks. I looked across the line. Charlie had his reins clenched in his teeth, all were leaning forward in their saddles with about 200 yards to go. Marcus "Cogburn" had both guns pointed toward the geese; his little mare had her ears forward seemingly waiting for the signal to charge! The breeze was perfect. It was coming from us to them giving us a little edge on the takeoff. A little further and they were starting to make a lot of noise. This was it! We were ready! I saw one flap its wings and hollered CHARGE! Away we went! We caught the geese by surprise and by the time they started to take off, we were about 50 yards away and closing fast. I guess they'd never seen a cavalry charge before!

That's when the casualties began. The first was Jerry. When his horse took off, his saddle slid back and the back cinch flanked his horse, giving him a reason to buck and unload Jerry. Next up was Henry whose horse also thought a little rodeo would be fun. Henry dropped his gun and stayed mounted. Instead of stopping and getting his gun, he got his rope down. "With that many geese, I should be able to catch at least one!" — and forward he went!

Just like that, we were amongst 'em. Marcus Cogburn was deliberate with his shots, alternating left and right hand shots with deadly accuracy. Claude dropped one and as he was loading a shell in his gun, he was knocked out of the saddle by another falling goose. Thanks, Charlie! I was enjoying the show so much that I'd nearly forgotten I even had a gun! I was able to drop two with one shot and scored with my next two shots.

Here came Jerry! He was able to get back into the action after all. He ended up getting one of the stragglers as we all ended up on the far side of where the flock was before the charge. Suddenly, Charlie's horse went down in a hole. Charlie went sprawling just as a man popped up out of the ground next to him dressed in camo with a shotgun in his hands, running for his life! Jason!

Meanwhile, Henry did actually rope a goose and was having quite a time of it. The goose was flying around above him and his horse wasn't liking it one bit! Jerry offered to shoot it, but Henry didn't want to take the chance of ruining a good rope. He ended up getting off his horse and reeled it in while on the ground.

We caught Charlie's horse and saw that Charlie's teeth were still clamped in the reins! To say that Charlie was unhappy was an understatement. We checked him and his horse over and decided that they were no worse for wear. Charlie was pretty easy going but I saw a look in his eyes that frankly scared me. He put his teeth in his shirt pocket, swung up on his horse and was getting his rope down while on his horse and at a dead run headed for Jason.

His loop flew true and Jason's feet were jerked out from under him and his gun went flying. By then, Henry showed up and put an insurance loop on him, but not until Charlie dragged him around for a hundred yards or so.

"You must be the sorry @#*#*@ that's been digging holes all over in my fields!" said Charlie. Starting right now, you're going to start filling them back up!"

"I didn't dig those pits and you can't make me fill them up!"

"How much is that shotgun of yours worth?" Jason looked a little worried.

"I paid $5000 for it and if it's damaged you'll be buying me a new one! Now give it back!"

"You'll get it back after all the holes are filled in. Until then, I'll keep it in a safe place."

"That's theft! I'll file charges against you as soon as I get back to town!

"If you don't get to work right away, it's going to be a long time before you even see town. You left your cell phone in the pit along with some other interesting stuff."

About that time they could see two trucks driving toward them. One was Bud and the other was the sheriff. "Here comes the sheriff! You guys are in trouble now!"

Bud, the sheriff, and Marcus' sister got out and came over to us.

"Sheriff, these guys stole my shotgun and are illegally detaining me"!

"Looks to me like they just caught a trespasser," he said with a serious look. "So far, you're looking at 3rd degree criminal trespass, vandalism, reckless discharge of a dangerous weapon, and abandoning or failure to properly care for wild game meat. That's just the beginning. Let me see that shotgun. Is this your gun Jason?"

"Yes it is, and these guys…"

"I see that it doesn't have the plug in it that's required to hunt waterfowl with. I also see that it has six rounds in the magazine. Two more charges against you."

Jason was starting to look sick. He looked even worse when the sheriff told him that everything involved in the crimes he'd committed could be confiscated, including his truck and shotgun if he didn't cooperate.

"I'll call my dad! He'll take care of this and get me out of here!"

"I've already called him; he's on his way right now."

It wasn't much longer before Jason's dad showed up and it was pretty evident where Jason got his arrogant attitude from. It didn't last very long, though, after the sheriff explained that he *(dad)* was responsible for his minor son.

Bud and Charlie decided to drop all charges with the stipulation that Jason fill in every pit blind on the property within two weeks. Also, Jason and his dad had to PLUCK all the geese we'd gotten that day according to our satisfaction. There wasn't a pin feather left on any of them and it took them all day long to finish but it was worth the wait! Jason still had to answer for the wildlife violations though. That was a different matter.

Oh, and another thing. Marcus' sister did a great job of capturing it all on video and it went viral on her YouTube channel. Now, we're all YouTube Stars! Since then, we've been told that this has become the latest rage, goose hunting from horseback! The Homecoming dance should be a lot of fun since SHE asked ME! Best goose hunt EVER!

CHAPTER 19

The Battle

Since all good stories begin with "Once upon a time," that's how I'll begin this one, but the difference between this story and others is…this one actually happened.

Once upon a time, in a place far, far away (*but maybe not so far away as you might think*), there was a king. His kingdom was so large as to be incomprehensible as to its vastness. No other kingdom was ever half so large as his. It was said that the people that lived there outnumbered the grains of sand in the sea, there were so many.

The King was very wise. In fact, to this day no one has ever been able to equal his wisdom and knowledge. All the people in the Kingdom respected this, but what was really incredible was that the King knew every person in his kingdom. And because he knew them, he also loved them. It didn't matter to him that some were tall while others were short. Some were intrigued by mechanics while others sat and listened to some discuss math and physics and watched while some told stories or explained unexplainable things about the universe. The variety of people was endless…just like the love the King had for all his people.

The King was very concerned with the happiness and teaching of his people. They needed to learn all the things that would bring them happiness, and at the same time, be able to practice these things on their own. They needed to develop talents and abilities that required different experiences to uncover. They needed not only to trust their loving King, but also to develop trust and confidence in themselves and in others. As great as this kingdom was, it just wasn't the place to accomplish these things and the King knew it. Each of them were going to need to attend the University for Advanced Studies along with a field trip where they could practice their new skills and where the most difficult tests were yet to be given if they were to continue to progress.

When the people were told of this opportunity, they shouted for joy! They shouted so much and so vigorously that the heavens shook and some of the stars fell out of their places creating a light show that had never been seen before as they collided with each other! The Northern Lights displayed a show of such magnitude with their glowing green and yellow curtains that they were seen as far south as Argentina!

Now, since there were so many people and a very limited amount of space in the University, the people had to wait their turn and prepare for when each would be able to go. Excitement was everywhere. "What are the tests going to be like? What kinds of tests are there and how often? How long is the field trip? WHAT IS a field trip?" were the general questions of the day. Others were concerned that they would miss friends and family. Some even wanted to know about the risks. Risks? What risks?!

Ah, the risks. The good King explained that all learning involves a certain degree of risk. Whether it be proper application of a new found knowledge or task or not following directions correctly. There is always risk. Every action has a consequence or a reward depending on the choices made. This posed a challenge to the people. Of course, the King knew and anticipated it long before any in the Kingdom had even considered it.

He outlined His plan for the kingdom and explained the opportunities for growth that all would have. They would all be allowed the freedom to choose what they wanted to do. A mediator would be chosen for those who made mistakes that they couldn't fix. Since none were perfect, that would include everyone.

"As you attend the University and apply what you learn on the field trip, you will make mistakes," said the King. " There will be tutors along the way whose job it is to help you when this happens and also to help keep you from making more mistakes. It won't be easy. Actually, it will be very difficult for most. But, when you succeed, you will have a kingdom of your own and have everything the King has."

Lots of cheers! This is a great idea!

"Those who follow the rules and listen to the tutors will do well. Those who don't, will end up in another kingdom."

More cheers and more concerned looks.

The King's first son said that we should be allowed the freedom to choose many of the courses the we were to take. Everyone cheered! They liked freedom! Freedom was great! Then came the risks. With this freedom comes responsibility for the choices made. More cheers, however not quite as many.

"I will help all who follow the Kings plan," said the first son. "No one will be left alone to fail if you heed the counsel given by the King".

Another son stepped up and announced his plan. "Who among you like it here?"

Everyone cheered!

"Who among you would like to have their own kingdom without the risks the other plan has?"

Lots of cheers with some curious looks. "Maybe it won't be as hard as we thought it was going to be—" some were thinking.

"I have a plan that ensures that every one of us ends up a winner and that no one loses a thing! Just think of it, NO RISKS!"

More cheers and a lot of concerned looks. Many stole glances at the King, but he sat on his throne with an unreadable, impassive face. As the second son outlined his plan, a look of astonishment and even fear came upon the faces of many of the people.

"This man wants to take away our freedom!," one man said.

"He wants to make us all his slaves," said another.

"No, he wants us all to return without any of us getting lost or failing!" And then," He wants all of US to worship HIM!"

No risks...no freedom...The debate went on until the King quietly stood up. A reverent hush came over the crowd as they looked expectantly to their loving king. After quickly and thoroughly reviewing both plans so that even the youngest of all could understand them, he made this simple declaration,"I will choose the first."

With that statement, pandemonium broke out. Those who were for the second son's plan quickly formed a group. "There are too many of us for the King to ignore! We will have our way!," said the second son. "Follow me and I will be the King!"

A look of complete astonishment fell on all the others. Nothing like this had ever happened in this happy and peaceful kingdom before. Those following the second son were now called rebels. They had rebelled against the good and fair King. The King tried to help them to understand that the direction they were taking was very dangerous and would have long lasting, even eternal consequences if they didn't change. Instead of heeding the King's counsel, they declared war on the King and his Kingdom. The ensuing battle was terrible.

Fully one third of the Kingdom were rebels. Notwithstanding the great numbers of rebels, the Kingdom prevailed and drove them out, the rebels never to return, never to enjoy the peace and happiness that had been theirs as long as any could remember. It was a sad time in the Kingdom. A very sad time...but it was also a time for rejoicing. The University was ready for the first students and anticipation was running high in the Kingdom.

As I said in the first of this narrative-story-saga, the University was far away. It was in a land all to itself. In fact, it was literally far from all other land. It was called Earth. The Field Trip is our life on this earth. This story is about you, me and everyone else that has been here on this earth and all who will yet come. We chose the plan of the older son while the rebels chose the other son's plan.

We are taught by many "tutors". Parents, good friends and Church leaders are examples of some of the tutors we encounter during our field trip, among many others. Here we encounter the risks that the oldest son told us about. His name is Jesus. He knew we would make mistakes that would keep us from returning home, so He made an atonement in our behalf. That makes it possible for us to overcome our mistakes with the help of Jesus Christ. He also gave us a "roadmap" so to speak...the scriptures. They teach us how to live and the things we need to know to go back home to God and His kingdom.

The other brother? He and his followers were cast out of the Kingdom, we knew that. But, they were cast down here to Earth to test and challenge us. They want to destroy us. They will never have a physical body of their own. They want ours. We know the other brother's name is Satan, the enemy of all things good, pure and happy.

One of the leaders in the fight against the rebels was chosen as the first student. He was a strong and valiant man. A man of impeccable courage and character. His name was Michael, as in Michael the Archangel, but we call him Father Adam.

Supporting scriptures: Jeremiah 1:5, Job 32:8, 38:4-7, Isaiah 14:12-15, Ecclesiastes 12:7, Zechariah 12:1, Hebrews 12:9, Jude 6, Luke 10:18, Romans 8:14-17, Acts 17:28-29, Revelations 12:4, 7-9, Psalms 82:6, John 10:33-34.

About the Author

Layne isn't really much of an author. He's just an average guy who dabbles in lots of different things and this book happens to be a compilation of stories, some true and others just for fun. He and Pam, his wife of over 34 years, live on their ranch in northwest Colorado, 12 miles outside of town where Layne is the fourth generation on the ranch.

They enjoy the solitude their home affords them as well as the freedom the surrounding countryside offers. They share the property with deer, elk, coyotes, bobcats, bears, beavers, muskrats, waterfowl, turkeys, and currently four horses.

Layne makes all kinds of things out of antlers ranging from whistles and black powder measures to finger rings, bolo ties, checkers and even a chess set. He creates handcrafted knives from blades their son Landon, owner of Bookcliff Knives, makes in addition to barbecue forks, steak turners, hoof picks and other items out of steel. He and Pam enjoy going to mountain man rendezvous where they offer their goods for sale.

They are active in their church, the Church of Jesus Christ of Latter-Day Saints, and appreciate truth and freedom wherever it's found.

Made in the USA
Middletown, DE
19 August 2022